WHY CAN'T I STOP?

RECLAIMING YOUR LIFE FROM A BEHAVIORAL ADDICTION

WHY CAN'T I STOP ?

JON E. GRANT, JD, MD, MPH, BRIAN L. ODLAUG, PhD, MPH, AND SAMUEL R. CHAMBERLAIN, MD, PhD

JOHNS HOPKINS UNIVERSITY PRESS • *Baltimore*

© 2016 Johns Hopkins University Press
All rights reserved. Published 2016
Printed in the United States of America on acid-free paper
2 4 6 8 9 7 5 3 1

Johns Hopkins University Press
2715 North Charles Street
Baltimore, Maryland 21218-4363
www.press.jhu.edu

Library of Congress Cataloging-in-Publication Data

Names: Grant, Jon E., author. | Odlaug, Brian L., author. | Chamberlain, Samuel, author.
Title: Why can't I stop? : reclaiming your life from a behavioral addiction / Jon E. Grant, JD, MD, MPH, Brian L. Odlaug, PhD, MPH, and Samuel R. Chamberlain, MD, PhD.
Description: Baltimore : Johns Hopkins University Press, 2016. | Series: A Johns Hopkins Press health book | Includes bibliographical references and index.
Identifiers: LCCN 2015030253| ISBN 9781421419657 (hardback) | ISBN 9781421419664 (paperback) | ISBN 9781421419671 (electronic)
Subjects: LCSH: Compulsive behavior. | Psychology, Pathological. | BISAC: HEALTH & FITNESS / General. | SELF-HELP / Substance Abuse & Addictions / General. | PSYCHOLOGY / Psychopathology / Addiction.
Classification: LCC RC533 .G723 2016 | DDC 616.85/84—dc23 LC record available at http://lccn.loc.gov/2015030253

A catalog record for this book is available from the British Library.

Special discounts are available for bulk purchases of this book. For more information, please contact Special Sales at 410-516-6936 or specialsales@press.jhu.edu.

Johns Hopkins University Press uses environmentally friendly book materials, including recycled text paper that is composed of at least 30 percent post-consumer waste, whenever possible.

CONTENTS

PREFACE

This book is for people who have behavioral addictions and for their families and friends. While drug and alcohol addictions may be difficult to miss, behavioral addictions commonly go unnoticed, and many people with these problems suffer in the shadows. A person with a behavioral addiction may be addicted to shopping, gambling, stealing, or playing games on the Internet. The behavior is one that becomes time consuming and, often, life disrupting.

We wrote this book to help people who have these problems and to help the family and friends of those with these problems. The information and guidance provided here is designed to bring readers closer to dealing with the often complicated issues surrounding these addictions. We hope readers will find the information useful as a first step in learning about behavioral addictions and in helping themselves or a loved one gain control over behaviors that are distressing to them.

Please note that all the cases in this book are fictionalized. Cases do not portray real patients or families but rather are based on our clinical experience with these conditions.

WHY CAN'T I STOP?

I

Introduction

At some point in our lives, we all engage in behaviors that are risky or unwise—behaviors that, deep down, we know are not rational. We might gamble on the lottery even though we know that, statistically, the odds are firmly against us; or we might impulsively buy some clothing or a gadget after getting our paycheck, never to remove it from its packaging. Why do we do this? In part we do it because these behaviors can be exciting and temporarily rewarding. They may allow us to forget about life's problems for a short time. Often, we think we can control our behaviors: we allow ourselves the occasional indulgence because we think of it as just a "splurge" or reward for ourselves.

It is increasingly recognized, however, that certain behaviors, such as gambling and shopping, have the potential to become addictive. Just as substances such as alcohol and narcotics are rewarding and habit forming, so too are some behaviors. For people with behavioral addictions, a once relatively benign behavior can escalate, leading them to spend inordinate amounts of time preparing for or engaging in the habit, while neglecting other areas of life. These repetitive habits persist even though the person experiences negative consequences. Eventually many people find that they no longer have any conscious control over the behavior.

One man told us, "I wish I could stop, but I just can't. It's like I have no control. How can that be? It's so frustrating."

As human beings, we pride ourselves on being able to control our behaviors. Whether in the arena of exercise, financial budgeting, or faithfulness to a partner, discipline is regarded as an enviable trait, and with greater discipline comes greater respect for ourselves and respect from others. Therefore, people who develop behavioral addictions can experience a great deal of emotional distress, including guilt and shame. John, a compulsive gambler, said, "I feel so ashamed because I've lost so much money, built up credit card debt, and have no savings left. How can I put my kids through college now?" Kate, who experiences irresistible urges to steal from local clothing stores, said, "I take things I don't even need. Afterward I regret it, but I can't take them back. I feel so worthless." Over the years of treating people who have behavioral addictions, we have heard one comment repeatedly: "I run a business, manage a family, and control myself in so many ways. Why can't I control *this* behavior?"

Behavioral addictions are frequently hidden from friends, family, and partners. Kate, who compulsively steals from shops, works as a lawyer and has a family: "To everyone else, I have a successful job and happy family—two kids, a loving husband, and a dog. I think people would be amazed to know that I steal. To be honest, I don't understand why I do it." Andrew, who was addicted to the Internet, described his behavior in this way: "My friends teased me that I wasn't going out any more. Some of them just moved on and found other friends, forgetting me. Others asked what was wrong, but what could I tell them? 'I'm addicted to the Internet'? It's only when I got depressed because of my Internet addiction that they noticed and encouraged me to get help from my family doctor."

When severe, behavioral addictions can significantly impair people's ability to function, whether in personal relationships, work, or finances. Because of these profound consequences, ultimately individuals may not be able to hide the addiction, despite their best efforts to cover it up. John had built up huge debts, the family home was at risk of being foreclosed, and his wife eventually saw the threatening legal letters. Kate's work had been suffering because of the amount of time she had been spending in stores. Every time she stole something, she risked catastrophic consequences. If discovered, she could get a criminal record, be forced to pay a fine, ruin her career, and suffer damage to her social and family relationships. Effectively, although Kate appeared fine, she was at the brink of losing everything. Things came to a climax when a store clerk caught Kate stealing something and called the police.

When other people find out about a friend's, relative's, or partner's behavioral addiction, they may not know how to respond or cope. They can have a profound sense of helplessness in watching a loved one suffer from a behavioral addiction. They may find that their attempts to help don't help—or even seem to make matters worse. Mary discovered that her husband had been going to the casino on nights when he told her he would be away on a business trip: "First I felt angry and betrayed. Then I wondered if he'd been gambling because he didn't love me anymore, and I wondered if gambling was just an excuse he used when in fact he was having an affair. He wasn't. With time, I found out more and more about his gambling addiction and that it is a recognized condition. I had no idea what to do to help, even though I wanted to."

Behavioral addictions impair function, can have legal and financial repercussions, and can lead to mental health issues such as depression and thoughts of suicide, as Andrew experienced: "I found myself getting stuck online using social media. I got so obsessed with other people's lives, I forgot about my own. In the end I was spending so much time online avoiding life that I became depressed. At times I felt like ending my life." Susan, a young woman, picked at her face compulsively, and her face got so scarred that she did not want to leave her home: "I hate myself for doing it, but while I am doing it, I enjoy it. Afterward I am so ashamed of myself and can't leave the house for several days. I can't go on living this way."

These conditions can be difficult for other people to understand. One common question asked of people with behavioral addictions is "Why don't you just stop?" But sufferers cannot just stop—at some point the behavior has become ingrained, compulsive, and, frequently, beyond their control. As we explain later in this book, recent research shows that behavioral addictions have a physical basis in the brain: evolutionarily, ancient parts of the human brain involving reward and reinforcement can become overactive, while brain regions responsible for exerting control over our habits and impulses do not work as they should. These neural imbalances perpetuate the behavior. Understanding these mechanisms helps researchers and physicians develop better treatments and may help explain why sufferers cannot "just stop," even though they want to.

With the exception of Internet addiction, these behaviors have been recognized for centuries. Dice have been discovered in caves dating back to around 3500 BC. Gambling has been recognized and, because of its addictive potential, regulated in many ancient cultures, including in China, Egypt, and Rome. The potential problems associated with gambling are described in ancient religious texts such as the Koran of Islam (~600 CE) and the Talmud of Judaism (~400 CE). Stealing is as ancient as the existence of personal possessions, and compulsive sexual habits have probably existed for just as long, reflecting a deeply ingrained primal drive. Consuming excessive quantities of food (related to our modern concept of food addiction) was documented in the Middle Ages as a practice among wealthy families, when members engaged in deliberate vomiting as a consequence of overeating.

Although these behaviors have been documented throughout history, the extreme forms have been recognized as uncontrollable problems, or "disorders," only since the nineteenth century. The term *kleptomania*, referring to compulsive stealing, was coined around 1816, when an apparent epidemic of young women stealing clothes in Paris was described in local newspapers. These women stole even though they did not need the items, and even though they had plenty of money to buy them. What we now call compulsive sexual behavior was described in the late 1700s as *nymphomania* (for females) and *satyrism* (for males), in people considered to have an overactive sex drive and excessive sexual activity. Compulsive shopping as a concept dates back to nineteenth-century America or earlier, referred to at that time as *oniomania*. Excessive grooming behaviors were first considered mental health problems during the nineteenth century too, with the medical community at a loss for how to explain these behaviors and what to do about them. Internet addiction is a more controversial concept that by definition only arose following the development of the Internet, from about 1970 onward.

As we explore in more detail throughout this book, various behavioral addictions are now formally recognized by the psychiatric profession, which has developed specific diagnostic criteria and treatments. Gambling, stealing, and grooming behaviors are all listed in the *Diagnostic and Statistical Manual of Mental Disorders,* fifth edition (*DSM-5,* American Psychiatric Association), which is used by mental health professionals to diagnose mental illnesses. In recognition of gambling's strong similarities to substance addiction, it was included in the category with drug and alcohol addiction. More and more people with other behavioral addictions are being seen by health care workers in clinical settings, but not all addictions have been formally recognized by the American Psychiatric Association because further research is needed: these addictions include compulsive sexual behavior, food addiction, compulsive shopping and buying, and Internet addiction.

Although they are often overlooked by health care providers and the media, behavioral addictions are remarkably common across the world. Research estimates that 10 to 15 percent of the population will have experienced one or more behavioral addictions over the preceding year (up to 48 million people in the United States alone). These conditions occur in both men and women, in all socioeconomic classes, and in all cultures.

Why do we focus on gambling, stealing, shopping and spending, food, sex, Internet use, hair pulling, and skin picking in this book? We focus on these categories of behavior because they are particularly rewarding and therefore likely to become the basis of an addiction. Other types of behavior—such as setting fires, nail biting, exercise, and tanning—may all have rewarding properties, but they are either relatively rare (fire setting) or simply less well studied (nail biting, exercise, tanning) than the behaviors considered in this book.

In our experience treating patients, we have seen that behavioral addictions can be among the most distressing but neglected of mental health conditions. We wrote this book with a view to helping people who experience these behavioral addictions but also their partners, relatives, and friends. We begin in the next chapter by outlining what is meant by "behavioral addiction" and describing the different categories of treatment and how family and friends can help. In the subsequent chapters we consider different behavioral addictions, with an emphasis on how they are diagnosed, how many people are affected, who tends to be affected, and what treatments are available. These chapters about individual behavioral addictions include fictionalized case examples from our clinical experience treating sufferers and the people in their lives.

In this book we also present what is known about the causes of these behaviors, including genetic and environmental factors, and the role of particular brain circuitry. The final chapter provides practical step-by-step advice for partners, friends, and family to best support and help loved ones who have behavioral addictions. At the end of the book you will find a list of resources around the world for people with these behaviors who are seeking more information or treatment. We also list some further reading on each topic, as we are aware that no single book can address all the issues of very complex behaviors.

We wrote this book because, although much is known about these behaviors, little information is available for those who struggle with them or for their loved ones. Our goal is to allow people with these behaviors to recognize that what they struggle with is not uncommon and that there is hope.

2

What Does Behavioral Addiction Mean?

Jeremy realized he had a problem controlling his use of Internet pornography. It was starting to destroy his work life and his marriage because he spent so much time on the Internet that his wife had started to distrust him. He went to see a therapist about the problem and was told he had a behavioral addiction. How could this be? He had never had problems with drinking, drugs, smoking, or gambling (the four classic addictions that came to mind). Why was he being grouped with people who had drug problems? He was both upset and embarrassed by the diagnosis.

Elizabeth started stealing when she was 15 years old, and by the time she was in her early thirties, she knew she needed help for her behavior. Her therapist told her that the behavior was similar to cocaine addiction, with the intense highs from the behavior of stealing and the almost constant urge to engage in it. Elizabeth had never used drugs before, but she found this explanation comforting and understandable. "I knew my behavior was not exactly the same as cocaine addiction, but the idea at least gave me a basic understanding of what I was going through and helped my family understand it. After all, we have all known drug-addicted people, but how many kleptomaniacs have any of us known?"

Should we use labels, and if so, which ones?

The term *addiction* carries with it many strong feelings. Although we are aware that addiction is a brain disease, we also need to admit that there is substantial social stigma associated with the term. The same can be said about *behavioral addictions*. Jeremy's reaction to his diagnosis is not uncommon. Many people are upset when the label *addiction* or *addict* is applied to them. They feel that they are being judged by the term.

In general, we are not advocates of using these labels. Elizabeth's case, however, shows that some people find it helpful to understand how these behaviors compare to drug addiction; even so, the term and the idea need to be explained and discussed. We use the term *behavioral addiction* throughout this book to be consistent in our use of language, but we caution that the people we treat and those described in this book are people, not labels or diagnoses.

A related issue is whether *behavioral addiction* is the best term for what we discuss in this book. Readers may have heard the terms *process addictions, non-substance addictions,* or *impulse control disorders,* which are also used to describe these problems. We have chosen *behavioral addictions* because it is currently used the most frequently and is used throughout the world.

What is a behavioral addiction?

Ingesting drugs and alcohol may produce short-term rewards that then result in a lack of control over the behavior. Several behaviors similarly produce short-term rewards and result in a lack of control over the behavior. Diminished control is a core defining concept of substance addiction. This similarity between the behaviors we discuss in this book and substance addiction has given rise to the concept of behavioral addictions. The idea of behavioral addictions is based in scientific knowledge, but the concept is still controversial.

How does someone get addicted to something without putting an addictive substance into the body? We now know that the brain can react to behaviors much as it does to drugs or alcohol. Certain behaviors produce a strong reinforcement in the brain that makes us want to do them over and over again, even if they interfere with our lives. The reinforcement of the behaviors can be so strong that some people go through withdrawal when they stop the behavior, just as in drug and alcohol addiction. They may become agitated, have trouble sleeping, undergo personality changes, and be irritable.

The scientific evidence of brain imaging, psychological assessments, and treatment that links these behaviors to substance addiction is strongest for gambling addiction, but the evidence is growing for the other behaviors discussed in this book. There are skeptics, though, and some of these skeptics are the people who struggle with the behaviors. "I don't think my hair-pulling problem is anything like someone who is addicted to drugs," someone might say. "Although I struggle with controlling the behavior, I don't think it's that bad." Keep in mind that there are levels of severity for any addiction. Although certain drug addictions lead to the complete devastation of people's lives, this does not mean that everyone with a drug addiction has the same level of problems. Similarly, some individuals with behavioral addictions may have significant consequences due to their behavior (such as bankruptcy, arrest, homelessness), but others function fairly well despite the behavior.

Skeptics of the idea of behavioral addiction further raise concern about whether mental health practitioners are simply making up disorders such as these to sell more pharmaceutical medications. Although we agree that some mental health problems are overdiagnosed, the behaviors we discuss in this book have been recognized for more than a century (with the obvious exception of Internet addiction). We are not proposing the introduction of new disorders but instead are recategorizing existing behaviors as a means of reflecting the scientific data, and with the hope of providing more effective treatment approaches.

Can any behavior be addictive?

The answer is probably "yes," depending on the person. Having said that, for this book we selected the behaviors that we and others see as having the strongest relationship to substance addictions. Although the pathological use of alcohol or drugs has been historically accepted as addiction, neuroscience research has now set the stage for an expanded definition of addiction. The fifth edition of the American Psychiatric Association's *Diagnostic and Statistical Manual of Mental Disorders* (DSM-5) officially recognized for the first time that behaviors could be regarded as forms of addiction. The *DSM-5*'s new chapter "Substance-Related and Addictive Disorders" includes gambling disorder, previously included with the "Impulse Control Disorders Not Elsewhere Classified." The disorder was relocated because of evidence showing that gambling and substance addiction have consistently high rates of co-occurrence (meaning they tend to occur together in the same person more often than would be expected by chance alone), similar presentations of some symptoms, and genetic and biological overlap. Biological overlap means that gambling and drugs of abuse appear to activate the same brain reward system, with similar effects.

Other behaviors may have similar effects on the brain's reward system, but they were either considered and rejected for inclusion in the *DSM-5* category of "Substance-Related and Addictive Disorders" (for example, Internet addiction and compulsive sexual behavior), were not even part of the debate (for example, food addiction, kleptomania, and compulsive buying), or were under consideration for a different grouping (the grooming disorders of trichotillomania [hair-pulling disorder] and excoriation [skin-picking] disorder were included as part of the "Obsessive Compulsive and Related Disorders" category).

Although mental health research is ongoing to understand the cause of these disorders, we still rely heavily on clinical symptoms to group disorders rather than having a full understanding of the problems in the brain itself. For example, some think compulsive sexual behavior should be grouped with other sexual problems instead of with addictions. Is it possible, however, that compulsive sexual behavior has similarities to substance addictions? If a small percentage of people with compulsive sexual behavior have brains similar to those of people with other sexual problems, and a large percentage have more in common biologically with people who have drug addiction, should compulsive sexual behavior be considered a sexual disorder or an addiction?

Even if we accept that certain behaviors (such as gambling) share some clinical and probably biological similarities to substance addiction, and even if we accept that grouping disorders is far from ideal, we are still left with deciding which disorders should be considered behavioral addictions. Our decisions for this book are rooted in two important points: first, based on the existing research, we include behavioral disorders that we believe have the strongest similarities to substance use disorders; and second, we are aware that not everyone with a particular disorder is similar to someone with a substance use disorder. Although we talk broadly about these disorders, we must stress that there is substantial variability within each disorder. That is, someone with gambling disorder may appear similar to someone with a substance addiction, while someone else with gambling disorder does not.

Pros and cons of grouping behaviors as behavioral addictions

Even before we present the research evidence showing how these behaviors are similar to substance addictions, we should also address the question of why we are interested in grouping these disorders together. As the two cases above illustrate, people with these behaviors might find this grouping informative, as did Elizabeth, or pejorative, as Jeremy viewed it, because of the stigma surrounding substance addictions.

What good could come from thinking of these behaviors as behavioral addictions rather than just as behaviors? To answer this, we must first acknowledge how little recognition of, or education about, these disorders occurs throughout most of the world. Some behavioral addictions have only recently been recognized by mental health experts (for example, Internet addiction and food addiction). Others go back years but have always had a mystery or stigma associated with them for various reasons: their criminal nature (kleptomania), their perceived immorality (compulsive sexual behavior), their perceived frivolity (compulsive buying), their perceived hedonism (gambling disorder), or their exotic nature (trichotillomania and skin-picking disorder, hereafter called trichotillomania or hair-pulling disorder interchangeably, and excoriation disorder or skin-picking disorder interchangeably). As a result, many people who struggle with these disorders have little or no understanding of their behaviors and lack meaningful language to use when explaining their behaviors to loved ones. Likening these disorders to substance addictions provides a common language, so people can begin to discuss and better understand these behaviors. Borrowing the terminology of addiction also communicates the out-of-control nature of these behaviors for many people as well as the personal and social costs associated with them. Finally, understanding these disorders from the perspective of substance addictions has allowed us to make important strides in treating the behaviors and may prove even more productive as time goes on.

Understanding these behaviors as addictions has some real downsides as well. First, the stigma of addiction—socially, personally, and morally—may be uncomfortable for people who struggle with these behaviors. Second, although substance addiction is a useful starting point, we know that many drugs of abuse have greater damaging effects to the brain over time than addictive behaviors do. Finally, treatments for substance addictions are not all useful for treating these behaviors. The behaviors themselves are not all equivalent, so grouping the disorders together and equating them to all addictions could mean overlooking the unique complexity of each disorder and lead us to assume that all should be treated in the same way. It could also lead us to consider certain treatment approaches (for example, those used to treat alcoholism) and ignore other potentially useful treatments (for example, seeing sexual compulsivity as a problem with intimacy).

Although we have chosen to group these disorders together for educational purposes and to develop a greater understanding of them, we stress that each disorder is unique and that even as a group, these are not simply the same as drug and alcohol addictions. Further, each individual with these behaviors is unique. When we discuss disorders, we need to keep in mind that generalities about disorders may or may not apply (or may apply in part) to the individual struggling with the behavior. The concept of behavioral addiction should be considered a starting point, rather than an end point, in trying to understand these behaviors.

How common are these behaviors?

The behavioral addictions we address in this book are, in fact, quite common. With the possible exception of kleptomania, the other disorders occur as often or more often than most mental health problems (see table 1). To put the prevalence rates in perspective, consider that disorders frequently mentioned in the news or popular press, such as schizophrenia, bipolar disorder, or anorexia nervosa, all have prevalence rates (1 percent, 0.8 percent, and 0.1 percent, respectively) lower than the prevalence rates for most behavioral addictions.

Couldn't other behaviors also be included?

Some researchers have argued that the category of behavioral addictions could be expanded beyond those presented here. For example, fire setting, excessive tanning, and compulsive exercise could be referred to as behavioral addictions as well. The only issue is that we simply do not have enough evidence currently to include these other behaviors. There has been ongoing interest in other behaviors such as these, but as you will see below, well-founded evidence should exist before additional behaviors are considered to be behavioral addictions. This idea leads to the question of whether any behavior could become addictive. There is

Table I *Lifetime Prevalence of Behavioral Addictions*

Behavioral Addictions	Lifetime Prevalence Rates
Gambling disorder	0.4% to 2.1%
Kleptomania (compulsive stealing)	0.4% to 0.9%
Compulsive sexual behavior	2.0% to 3.7%
Internet addiction	2.6% to 5.3%
Food addiction	5.0% to 8.0%
Compulsive buying	3.6% to 5.8%
Trichotillomania (hair-pulling disorder)	0.6% to 3.9%
Excoriation (skin-picking) disorder	1.4% to 4.2%

Note: Because most of these disorders have not been included in epidemiological surveys (with the exception of gambling disorder), these numbers are taken from various community surveys worldwide.

evidence that if a behavior activates the same reward system in the brain as substance addictions, then it could theoretically become addictive. This does not mean that *all* behaviors, however, can "turn on" this same system. Answers to these questions await more research.

What is the evidence that these behaviors are like substance addictions?

The term *addiction* was traditionally used in relation to specific psycho-active substances, such as cocaine, alcohol, and nicotine. Substances with addictive properties exert, to some extent, common effects on the brain's reward pathways, notably the area of the brain known as the *ventral striatum.* Core aspects of addiction include impaired control (for example, craving increasingly large quantities, unsuccessful attempts to reduce intake), functional impairment (for example, narrowing of interests, neglect of other areas of life), and risky use (continuing intake despite awareness of damaging psychological or physiological effects). The behavioral addiction model makes sense at face value: individuals with various behaviors (gambling, excess grooming, stealing, excess use of the Internet) seem to share remarkable clinical parallels to people with addictive substances, including impaired control, functional impairment, and persisting engagement in the behavior despite negative consequences. People may experience withdrawal-like symptoms when they try to stop a behavioral addiction, as do people with a substance addiction. Many of these behaviors (for example, gambling) seem to share more in common with traditional addictions, while the evidence linking others to substance addiction may seem less convincing (for example, trichotillomania and skin picking). With more scientific evidence constantly emerging, the links, or lack thereof, between each behavior and substance addiction will become clearer.

Clinical similarities

Behavioral and drug addictions share common core qualities: (1) repetitive or compulsive engagement in a behavior despite adverse consequences; (2) diminished control over the problematic behavior; (3) an urge or craving prior to engaging in the problematic behavior; and (4) a pleasurable experience during the performance of the problematic behavior. In both behavioral and substance addictions, the person is unable to resist the drive to perform some act that is harmful to the person.

Behavioral and substance addictions usually start in adolescence and young adulthood, although it may take years before the behavior becomes out of control. Both addictions also tend to be chronic, with the person stopping and starting the behavior on multiple occasions.

The rewarding nature (sometimes called "positive reinforcement") of behavioral addictions is similar to the experience of substance addictions. Both behavioral and substance addictions, however, may become less rewarding over time, and the person feels the *need* to do it instead of simply *wanting* to do it (sometimes called "negative reinforcement"). The person then engages in the behavior to avoid the negative consequences (such as withdrawal) associated with not doing the behavior.

Behavioral and substance addictions have other clinical similarities. People with behavioral addictions frequently report an urge or craving state prior to the behavior, as do individuals with substance addictions. Additionally, these behaviors often decrease anxiety and result in a positive mood state, or high, similar to what happens in substance intoxication. Emotional turbulence may contribute to cravings in both behavioral addictions and substance use disorders. Many people with behavioral addictions report a decrease in these positive mood effects with repeated behaviors and therefore a need to increase the intensity of behavior to achieve the same mood effect, which is like tolerance in substance addictions. Many people with behavioral addictions also report a negative or unpleasant mood while abstaining from the behaviors, analogous to withdrawal. (Unlike substance withdrawal, however, there are no reports of medically serious withdrawal states from behavioral addictions.) As in substance use disorders, financial, interpersonal, and health problems are common in behavioral addictions. Individuals with behavioral addictions, like those with substance addictions, may jeopardize their health and well-being to ensure that they can undertake their addictive behavior.

As in substance addictions, behavioral addictions usually begin in childhood or adolescence, with males tending to start at an earlier age. Although recently brought into question, a *telescoping phenomenon* has been extensively documented in various substance use disorders as well as in certain behavioral addictions. In telescoping, women have a later initial engagement in the addictive behavior but a shorter time from initial engagement to the development of addiction.

Similar personalities

Individuals with behavioral addictions and those with drug and alcohol problems all tend to score high on measures of impulsivity and sensation seeking. These are generally people who find it difficult to delay gratification. Those with behavioral addictions also score high on measures of compulsivity (predisposition toward repetitive engagement in a behavior).

Co-occurrence

Although most epidemiological studies have not included behavioral addictions, existing data support the idea that a relationship exists between certain behavioral addictions (gambling disorder, Internet addiction, compulsive sexual behavior, skin-picking disorder) and substance addictions (see table 2). In particular, gambling disorder increases the risk of having an alcohol problem, Internet addiction has also been associated with harmful alcohol use and cannabis use, and nicotine dependence and trichotillomania frequently co-occur. These findings suggest that behavioral addictions may share a common biology with substance addictions. In addition, a person who has one behavioral addiction is likely to have others as well.

Does having both a behavioral addiction and a substance addiction tell us anything about cause and effect? Substance and behavioral addictions may interact and perpetuate one another. For example, substance addictions may develop as a consequence of a behavioral addiction, or vice versa. Complicating this picture further is that a range of other psychi-

Table 2 *Lifetime Estimates of Substance Addictions in People Who Have Behavioral Addictions*

Behavioral Addictions	Lifetime Estimates of Substance Addictions
Gambling disorder	35% to 63%
Kleptomania (compulsive stealing)	23% to 50%
Compulsive sexual behavior	64%
Internet addiction	38%
Food addiction	20% to 25%
Compulsive buying	21% to 46%
Trichotillomania (hair-pulling disorder)	19%
Excoriation (skin-picking) disorder	38%

Note: Lifetime estimates of substance addictions in the population at large are approximately 30 to 40 percent.

atric disorders, such as major depressive disorder, bipolar disorder, obsessive-compulsive disorder, and attention deficit hyperactivity disorder, are also frequently reported in people with behavioral addictions. This *comorbidity* (having more than one medical problem) has raised the question of whether the relationship between behavioral and substance addictions is due to the person's biology, a complex relationship in which one behavior reinforces the other, or even some other underlying issues, such as an impulsive personality or early life stress, which may be the link to other disorders as well.

Cognitive similarities

Behavioral and substance addictions appear to share some common cognitive features. The behaviors that characterize both behavioral and substance addictions are impulsive. They are often premature, poorly thought out, and risky, and they result in negative long-term outcomes. Deficits in aspects of inhibition, working memory, planning, cognitive flexibility, and time management are more common in individuals with behavioral and substance addictions than in *healthy volunteers* (people without any psychiatric disorder). In particular, disordered gamblers and individuals with substance addictions more rapidly overlook, or become insensitive to, rewards, and they perform disadvantageously on decision-making tasks. A study of individuals with Internet addiction demonstrated no such deficits in decision making, providing another example of why we cannot think of all behavioral addictions as sharing the same underlying thought process.

Family history and genetics

Substance addictions frequently run in the families of those with behavioral addictions. Family studies of individuals with gambling disorder, trichotillomania, kleptomania, and compulsive buying have found that first-degree relatives (parents, children, siblings) are more likely to have alcohol or drug problems than first-degree relatives of people without behavioral addictions. These controlled family studies support the view that behavioral addictions may have a familial relationship to substance addictions.

Saying that something runs in families, however, does not necessarily say why. Is it because of an environmental factor, such as children modeling their behaviors based on their parents' behavior? Or is there a genetic relationship between behavioral and substance addictions (parents or other family history of drinking or other addictive problems)?

The genetic versus environmental contributions to specific behaviors and disorders can be estimated using twin studies, in which the risk of monozygotic (identical) twins sharing a given disorder is compared to the risk of dizygotic (nonidentical) twins sharing a given disorder. Research in male twins suggests that almost two-thirds (64 percent) of the co-occurrence between gambling and alcohol problems was attributable to genes that influence both behaviors, suggesting overlap in the genetics of both conditions.

Common biological processes

The excessive intake of drugs or alcohol likely causes multiple psychological, social, and biological disruptions. On the biological level, drugs and alcohol increase the chemical called dopamine, a *neurotransmitter*, in the brain's "reward system." In addition, drug and alcohol intoxication is associated with strong reinforcement effects. Continued drug or alcohol use is also associated with changes in the brain's neurotransmitters. Although the initial use of drugs or alcohol increases dopamine in the brain, the continued use results in diminished dopamine functioning, which is considered a hallmark of substance addiction. Another consequence of continued drug or alcohol use is that sights, locations, and people associated with the drug or alcohol become more important than sights, locations, and people associated with other activities. In essence, the brain's reward system becomes "hijacked" by drug- or alcohol-related environmental cues. In addition, over time and with chronic drug or alcohol use, the use becomes compulsive, which means that people with substance addiction have less ability to inhibit their drug- or alcohol-seeking behavior. It is thought that similar changes in the brain take place in behavioral addictions.

Several chemicals in the brain seem to play roles in behavioral addictions. Exactly how these chemicals function in behavioral addictions, and whether a particular person has a problem with a particular chemical, cannot be determined at this time. What we currently know is that any or all of these chemicals may be somewhat dysfunctional in people with behavioral addictions. Dopamine is implicated in learning, motivation, and rewards. Another chemical, glutamate, may be an important factor in impulsivity, craving, and relapse. Low levels of another neurotransmitter, serotonin, in the brain have been associated with high levels of impulsivity and sensation seeking. Noradrenaline is involved in arousal, excitement, and sensation seeking, while the opioid system is believed to play a role in urges, reward, and pleasure.

Brain imaging research has also demonstrated that behavioral addictions have a strong relationship to drug and alcohol addiction. Brain imaging has looked at both the driving forces of these behavioral addictions and the ability of people with these behaviors to control their impulses. Areas of the brain involved in drive or reward are implicated in both substance addictions and certain behavioral addictions. In addition, the part of the brain that helps control our impulsive decision making (the frontal part of the brain) appears to play a part in behavioral and substance addictions. For example, in those addicted to Internet gaming, the brain regions stimulated by Internet games (orbitofrontal, dorsolateral prefrontal, anterior cingulate, nucleus accumbens) are the same regions we see stimulated in people with drug addictions when they get "turned on" by drug triggers. Similarly, individuals with compulsive sexual behavior exhibit greater brain activation in the dorsal anterior cingulate cortex, nucleus accumbens, and amygdala than individuals without any mental health problems when viewing erotic videos.

We have also learned about the biology of behavioral addictions from research in Parkinson's disease. Between 6 and 10 percent of people with Parkinson's disease have reported developing a new behavioral addiction (such as gambling, stealing, sex, overeating) when they were taking medications that enhance dopamine transmission in the brain's reward pathways. Genetic or environmental predispositions to the development of an addiction in these individuals may be factors, along with the introduction of the dopamine agonist, which activates dopamine receptors in the brain.

These findings suggest an overlapping biology between substance addictions and behavioral addictions: the strongest evidence to date is for an overlap between substance addiction and gambling disorder, but the lack of evidence for other behavioral addictions may simply reflect the smaller amount of research into other behavioral addictions. Clearly behavioral addiction is not "one thing." Some of the biological abnormalities in behavioral addictions may mean a person is vulnerable to developing the addiction rather than that biology changes because of the addiction.

Similarities in response to treatment

Behavioral and substance addictions respond positively to the same or similar treatments. The twelve-step self-help approaches, motivational enhancement, and cognitive behavioral therapies commonly used to treat substance addictions have been successfully used to treat gambling disorder, compulsive sexual behavior, kleptomania, Internet addiction, and compulsive buying. Psychotherapy for both behavioral and substance addictions often relies on a relapse prevention model that encourages abstinence by identifying patterns of abuse, avoiding or coping with high-risk situations, and making lifestyle changes that reinforce healthier behaviors.

Despite how many people are affected by behavioral addictions worldwide, no medications are currently approved for treating them. Some medications that have shown promise in treating substance addictions, however, have also shown promise in treating behavioral addictions. Naltrexone, a medication that blocks the opiate system in the brain and thereby reduces urges for addictive behaviors, is approved by the U.S. Food and Drug Administration (FDA) for the treatment of alcoholism and opioid dependence. This medication has shown benefit in treating gambling, compulsive sexual behavior, compulsive buying, food addiction, skin picking, and trichotillomania. Similarly, medications that alter the activity of the chemical glutamate, which is involved in reward and urges, have been used successfully to treat both behavioral addictions and substance dependence. Topiramate, a medication approved for seizures, has shown promise for gambling, compulsive buying, kleptomania, trichotillomania, and skin-picking disorder; it is also effective in reducing alcohol, cigarette, and cocaine use. N-acetylcysteine, an amino acid that a person can buy at a health food store without prescription, reduces hair-pulling and skin-picking behaviors as well as gambling urges and behavior. It also reduces cocaine cravings and use as well as marijuana use. Finally, memantine, a medication used to treat Alzheimer's disease, may reduce drinking, cigarette smoking, intravenous heroin use, gambling, shopping, and stealing. Studies suggest that by understanding what works for treating substance addiction, we can gain insights into promising treatment options for behavioral addictions as well.

Aren't these behaviors just OCD or symptoms of depression or anxiety?

Many people with behavioral addictions have been told that they have a form of obsessive-compulsive disorder (OCD). OCD is a mental disorder in which people experience repetitive intrusive thoughts (obsessions) and/or repetitive compulsive mental acts or physical rituals (compulsions). For example, individuals with OCD might experience intrusive obsessional thoughts that they have contaminated their hands with germs and, in response, will repeatedly wash their hands for hours on end in order to neutralize these thoughts.

Viewing behavioral addictions as forms of OCD is based on the common features of repetitive thoughts and behaviors. Certain clinical aspects, such as ritualistic behaviors, are shared between OCD and addictive behaviors (for example, gamblers often do things in a specific order to bring luck; many compulsive buyers excessively collect the things they purchase; kleptomaniacs may collect the things they steal). What's different between people with behavioral addictions and people with OCD are personality features and biological features. Personality features of individuals with behavioral addictions include being impulsive and seeking rewards and sensations, while people with OCD are typically harm avoidant. In terms of biological differences, increased activity in cortico-basal ganglionic-thalamic circuitry has been described in studies of OCD when symptoms are provoked, but relatively decreased activity has been observed in these brain regions in symptom provocation studies in gambling. Other than in people with trichotillomania (hair pulling) and excoriation (skin-picking) disorder, family studies have not demonstrated an association between most of the behavioral addictions and OCD. Thus, except perhaps with hair-pulling and skin-picking disorders, there is simply less evidence linking these behaviors to OCD than to substance addictions.

Many people report doing their addictive behavior when they are feeling down or stressed, so some researchers and physicians have wondered whether these behaviors are merely symptoms of depression or anxiety. People can engage in either rewarding behaviors or in behaviors that help them "zone out" when they are feeling depressed or anxious. Many people with behavioral addictions report that the pleasurable yet problematic behaviors alleviate negative emotional states. The elevated rates of co-occurrence between these behaviors and depression and anxiety could support a relationship between behavioral addictions and depression or anxiety, at least in some people. This may be why some people who have behavioral addictions respond to treatment with antidepressant medications.

Just as with substance addictions, however, depression in these behaviors may be distinct from primary or uncomplicated depression. For example, depression in behavioral addictions may be a response to shame and embarrassment arising from the specific behaviors of the behavioral addiction, such as stealing. In addition, the repetitive behavior of a behavioral addiction usually continues well after the person's depression or anxiety has cleared. This suggests that the behaviors are independent from anxiety and depression for most people, though they often coexist.

Misdiagnosis

As we have mentioned, many clinicians have little if any familiarity with these behaviors, even though they are very common. Because many health care providers are not familiar with behavioral addictions, they may incorrectly diagnose patients and prescribe treatment that is not useful or possibly even counterproductive. Therefore, patients and their families may have to educate their providers about these disorders. Individuals may be misdiagnosed as having depression instead of a behavioral addiction. Many people engage in all sorts of unhealthy behaviors to relieve, or "self-medicate," their depression, including, sometimes, sex, gambling, shopping, or unhealthy eating. If the behaviors exist when the person is not depressed, or if the behaviors possibly contribute to the depression, a behavioral addiction may be the primary problem.

Many clinicians misdiagnose the person with a behavioral addiction as having bipolar disorder. When people are *manic,* they feel euphoric, don't sleep, and act impulsively, and they may engage in activities that are pleasurable but have negative consequences. They do so because they are not able to judge the negative outcomes appropriately. Excessive gambling, sexual activity, and spending recklessly may all occur during a manic episode (assuming that other symptoms of mania also exist). If the problematic behavior also occurs when the person's mood is stable, the individual may have a behavioral addiction in addition to bipolar disorder. If this behavior (gambling, sexual activity, spending) is the only problematic one that the person exhibits and there are no other symptoms of mania, then the diagnosis of bipolar disorder is less appropriate than a diagnosis of behavioral addiction.

People are often told that the behavior is simply a symptom of anxiety. It's true that people who are worried and cannot stop thinking about possible catastrophic outcomes can find relief in distraction or in doing things that help them zone out and forget other problems. Hair pulling, skin picking, Internet use, gambling, sex, eating, and shopping can all provide this sort of transient relief from anxiety. When the behaviors occur or continue to occur even in moments of calm, when no anxiety is present, then they are likely to be independent problems that should be addressed as behavioral addictions.

Finally, because behavioral addictions often co-occur with substance addiction, some clinicians ignore the behavioral addiction and focus on the drug or alcohol problem only. Some people exhibit reckless, impulsive behaviors when intoxicated by alcohol or high on drugs. These individuals may gamble, have reckless sex, spend too much money, pick at their skin, pull their hair, or eat excessively. Alcohol intoxication is often disinhibiting, and people who are intoxicated or high may do things they would not ordinarily do. Stimulants, both prescribed and illicit (cocaine, methamphetamine), can also make people hypersexual and impulsive and can cause picking and pulling behaviors. Cannabis use may result in eating that is out of control. If these symptoms do not decrease or stop when the person is free from drugs and alcohol, then a diagnosis of behavioral addiction would be indicated.

What these behaviors are not

Although we discuss these behaviors as addictions, there is no evidence to support what many people refer to as an "addictive personality." People who come to see us often state that they are generally addictive in nature. This may be true, but they more likely have sensation-seeking or impulsive personalities rather than addictive ones. The distinction should be made because the "addictive personality" term suggests an overall unhealthy approach to behaviors. The more appropriate term, *impulsive personality*, instead suggests that the *drive* for many of these behaviors is not necessarily unhealthy but that the *intensity* of the behavior and *lack of control* over the behavior are the problems.

These behavioral addictions often involve illegal or socially unacceptable behaviors, such as stealing or sexual acts. Behavioral addictions are not, however, simply character flaws or moral weakness. This is often difficult for people and their families to accept. They seldom know other people who have these problems, and they cannot fully understand why someone engages in illegal or seemingly immoral behavior over and over again if they are not, in fact, morally flawed people. Yet research on the spiritual or religious qualities of people with these behaviors has found no differences between these people and those without these behaviors; people are no more likely to be "good" or "bad" just because they engage in these behaviors. Furthermore, the rewarding aspect of the behavior, not the immoral or illegal nature of it, seems to be the driving force. The reward could be multiple aspects of the behavior, such as the ability to acquire something (as in kleptomania) or the "naughty" factor (as in compulsive sexual behavior or kleptomania). Many people have stolen something from a friend or a store when they were young, and many young people have found sexual behaviors enticing, but they do not necessarily continue to engage in the behaviors when they grow up. Young people who engage in these behaviors are often testing boundaries and figuring out how to cope emotionally, rather than displaying behavioral addictions. They are not acting out of moral weakness. For some people, however, the behaviors are too rewarding and are extremely difficult to control.

The fact that most people can control their behavior while others cannot does not mean they are more or less moral; it may simply mean that the reward is greater for some than others. Although some people with behavioral addictions have personality difficulties and repeatedly engage in immoral behaviors, they do not seem to be more represented among people with behavioral addictions than among those without the addictions.

Further complicating the picture is that some very good people do some very bad things when a behavioral addiction is strong and leads to overwhelming problems. For example, people with gambling problems but no history of illegal behavior have embezzled from their jobs to pay off their gambling debt or to further fund their gambling behavior. People with compulsive sexual behavior have lied to spouses about extramarital affairs and have put their partners at risk of contracting HIV and other sexually transmitted infections. What does it say about someone who does something wrong when under extreme pressure? Is it simply that the behavioral addiction made them do it? Not everyone who gambles also embezzles, and not everyone who is compulsively sexual would put his or her partner at risk. So, did the pressure of the behavioral addiction unearth a deeper character flaw? These questions cannot be answered in the abstract but need to be examined on an individual basis. We do not excuse any related illegal or immoral behaviors, such as embezzlement or infidelity. They, as well as personality strengths and flaws, should all become a focus of treatment.

Case

Stephen developed a serious gambling problem in his early twenties. His gambling brought financial difficulties and led him to become estranged from his family and friends. When he told his primary doctor about his behavior, the doctor informed him that the gambling was probably due to his loneliness, and that Stephen should do more socially. Stephen's gambling continued, and he began stealing and pawning family heirlooms.

When Stephen came to our clinic, we spent part of his initial visit explaining the diagnosis of gambling disorder, exploring what we thought "caused" it, and talking about how it could be treated. When we discussed the similarities to substance addiction, Stephen instantly felt that he understood his behavior. He had known family members who struggled with alcoholism, and the parallel to his situation (in particular the insatiable "need" to gamble) seemed to fit his own struggles. With this information, Stephen no longer felt like some sort of outcast in the family. In addition, when treatments that mirrored those for alcoholism were presented to Stephen, he was motivated to get started.

Key Points for Individuals with Behavioral Addictions

1. Although there is evidence that behavioral addictions are often similar—clinically, biologically, and in treatment response—to drug and alcohol addiction for many people, this does not mean they are the same thing or that you are similar to everyone else with these problems.
2. Individuals with behavioral addictions are often misdiagnosed by health care providers as having some other problem. If the diagnosis does not seem correct to you, you should provide the clinician more information regarding the behavior, what drives it, and what you are thinking and feeling when you perform the behavior.

Key Points for Family Members

1. The diagnosis of a behavioral addiction is based on what the person tells the health care provider. Brain scans, tests for neuro-chemicals, and cognitive testing are still largely done only for research purposes. Because many people are embarrassed by the behavior, family members are extremely valuable in letting the health care provider know about the person's behavior. This helps the clinician make the correct diagnosis.
2. These are complicated problems. Family members are not to blame for the person's behavior, and it is important to avoid concluding that a person is "bad" morally because they undertake some acts that are questionable or hard to fathom.

3

Gambling

Marilyn is now 53 years old. She started gambling at the age of 50 after going to a riverboat casino with friends one Friday night. "I went with two friends for a night out, and I just loved it. Something about the casino made me forget my problems for a few hours, forget the troubles with my husband and son, and simply let me zone out." After going again a few times with friends, Marilyn began going to the casino by herself, monthly for a few months and then at least once a week. Initially, she was concerned about her behavior: "I thought, *Why am I doing this?* But I just couldn't stop going. I enjoyed it too much." After a few months, she no longer thought about why she was going, because her thoughts were preoccupied with gambling, gambling strategies, and how to get the money to gamble without her husband finding out what she was doing. She began lying to him about her whereabouts, saying that she had events at church, had to work late, or had plans with friends. After three years, however, she had to tell him the truth, because she had been using their communal funds and was now several months late in making mortgage payments.

Marilyn's husband urged her to get treatment for her gambling. She started weekly therapy, which lasted about ten months. The focus for therapy started with her gambling, but after three months, it was clear that Marilyn had issues within her marriage, and the therapy began focusing on that as well. Marilyn has been able to stay abstinent from gambling for many months, but problems within the marriage continue to wax and wane in intensity.

Why should we be concerned about gambling?

Gambling is everywhere and does not appear to be going away anytime soon. It is a lucrative industry, with United States casinos alone reporting annual gross revenues of more than $66 billion in 2013. If we add in the revenues from online gambling activities, another $10 billion annually, it is clear that gambling is here to stay.

Gambling is itself not necessarily a bad thing. Most people who gamble do so recreationally and report no significant financial consequences or any difficulties controlling their behavior. For some people, gambling is a positive experience—they get out among others, engage in a form of adult play, and generally do so responsibly.

Some people, however, develop a maladaptive form of gambling behavior associated with impaired functioning, reduced quality of life, and high rates of bankruptcy and divorce. This form of gambling behavior has been defined by the American Psychiatric Association, in its fifth edition of the *Diagnostic and Statistical Manual of Mental Disorders* (*DSM-5*), as "Gambling Disorder," a mental health problem. The idea of gambling becoming a problem for some people is not a new one. Gambling problems have been recognized for at least one hundred years by the medical community. In 2013, in *DSM-5*, the disorder was grouped with substance addictions because many people with gambling problems also have substance addictions, gambling addiction looks a lot like drug addiction (for example, inability to stop the behavior despite multiple problems, experiencing withdrawal symptoms when trying to stop), and gambling disorder seems to have some genetic overlap with drug and alcohol addiction (families whose members have substance addictions also often have members with gambling problems).

How is gambling disorder diagnosed?

Like other mental health disorders, gambling disorder cannot be diagnosed using a blood test. And though researchers talk about brain imaging findings in gamblers, there is no way to determine if someone has a gambling problem by doing a brain scan. At this point, the diagnosis is made by what people tell their doctor and what the family may also tell the doctor.

Family involvement is particularly important in helping to make the diagnosis. As with substance addictions, many people with gambling problems tend to downplay their problems, often telling the doctor that things are fine and that they are more than able to stop gambling if they choose to do so. This does not necessarily mean the person is lying; they have told themselves these stories so many times that they actually believe they do not have any (or much of a) problem with gambling.

Family members or other loved ones can provide valuable information that gives a clearer picture of the person's struggles with gambling. Yet family members often believe they cannot tell a doctor anything because of privacy issues. A patient's privacy prevents the doctor from discussing the patient's details with family or other loved ones, but family member and other loved ones can tell the doctor anything they like.

The essential feature of gambling disorder is persistent and recurrent maladaptive gambling behavior that results in psychosocial dysfunction. To be diagnosed with gambling disorder, an individual must have experienced at least four of the following nine symptoms during the same twelve-month period:

1. The person is preoccupied with gambling—thinking about gambling for at least one hour each day: for example, thinking about which casinos have the best payouts on slots or how to improve the odds of winning.
2. The person has increased the amount of money used to gamble in order to experience the same level of excitement—this is a lot like

the idea of tolerance that we see in drug and alcohol problems: for example, after several months, a person who used to gamble with fifty dollars during an evening would not even consider gambling with less than two hundred dollars.

3. The person has tried unsuccessfully to reduce or quit gambling— for example, the person promises his wife he will not gamble again, and he is able to stop for a few weeks but then breaks down and gambles again.

4. The person becomes restless when unable to gamble—this is a lot like withdrawal from alcohol or drugs; for many years, people were not convinced that gamblers withdraw when they try to quit gambling. As it turns out, about 30 to 40 percent of gamblers will experience withdrawal symptoms (restlessness, agitation, insomnia, irritability), and these withdrawal symptoms may last a few months after someone stops gambling.

5. The person gambles as a means of escaping an unpleasant feeling, such as anxiety or depression. We see this above, in Marilyn, who used gambling as a way to escape uncomfortable family stress.

6. The person keeps returning to gambling in an attempt to win money back—this is often called "chasing losses." Gambling is a unique problem in the sense that the person feels the answer to the problem is the behavior itself. For example, Marilyn gets into debt from gambling and then keeps gambling as a means of recouping her losses. The person is gambling because she wants to, but there is also an element of desperation in the gambling. When someone develops debt, say about thirty thousand dollars, what options are available for the person to repay the debt? Sometimes a second job may help, but gamblers believe that the only way to pay off that amount of debt is to "win big"—then they'll pay off the debt and quit gambling.

7. The person has been lying to people about the extent of the gambling. Lying and secrecy are major telltale signs of a gambling problem.

8. The person has jeopardized or lost a significant relationship or opportunity because of gambling. The person stops doing things with friends, for example, or is not doing well at work because of being late, tired, or preoccupied.
9. The person has had to rely on others to help with the financial problems caused by gambling.

Important aspects in making the diagnosis

Making the diagnosis of gambling disorder should be more than simply checking off the symptoms and saying "yes," the person has a gambling problem, or "no," the person does not have a gambling problem. The professional medical assessment of someone with gambling disorder should focus on the gambling behavior, related mental and physical issues, previous treatments, what the person has tried on his own to control the gambling, and what the person currently expects from treatment.

In terms of the gambling behavior, it is important to assess current gambling patterns, the functional effects of the gambling, the reason for currently seeking treatment, how the person thinks about his gambling (which may assist with planning cognitive behavioral therapy), and whether the person has urges to gamble (which may assist with choosing a pharmacological intervention). The evaluation must also include a detailed understanding of the extent of the gambling, the repercussions of the problem on the individual's life (for example, financial, social, psychological, and familial), the person's readiness for change, and his sense of control over the gambling.

Are there different levels of severity in a gambling disorder?

It is important to recognize that among individuals with gambling disorders, there are differences in the severity of the gambling behavior. Some people have a mild problem, while others have a severe problem with gambling. Treatment approaches depend on the overall severity of the gambling disorder. For example, the therapy may need to be extended for a longer duration, and medication may need to be considered as an augmentation to therapy, in moderate and severe cases.

What if the person has only a couple of gambling symptoms?

Experiencing a couple of symptoms but failing to have four symptoms to make the diagnosis of gambling disorder has historically been considered *problem gambling*, a level of behavioral problem slightly less than that of gambling disorder. This condition, too, can greatly impair a person's functioning and result in significant negative consequences. It should not be taken lightly. If the person is willing, we recommend treatment for this condition. The treatment is usually less intensive and goes on for a shorter time than the treatment used for full gambling disorder.

What about gambling in binges?

People who gamble in binges often do not recognize they have a problem because they may go stretches of time without gambling. This may make them believe they have control over the behavior, and to some extent, they do have control. Gambling in binges, however, may produce the same outcomes as regular gambling, with financial and personal devastation. Binge gambling should therefore be treated when the person meets criteria for a gambling disorder, even if the frequency comes and goes.

People with binge gambling may need longer treatment so they can see if the behavior has really changed. The length of treatment should be determined to coincide with the time frame of a few binges. For example, if individuals binge every three months and then go to treatment for two months, they may be fooled into thinking they are doing well. They will not know if the treatment is effective until after at least three months and would benefit from probably six to nine months of treatment.

The consequences of gambling

Gambling disorder significantly impairs a person's ability to function socially and occupationally. Many individuals report intrusive thoughts and urges related to gambling that interfere with their ability to concentrate at home and at work, and work-related problems such as absenteeism and poor performance are common. People often report thinking of gambling literally most of every day. These obsessive gambling-related thoughts make it difficult to focus on work-related tasks.

Many people who have gambling disorder also have marital problems, as well as diminished intimacy and trust within the family and other interpersonal relationships. These consequences of gambling frequently, and ironically, may then lead to more gambling: "If my spouse already doesn't trust me, I might as well gamble anyway." Because many men believe their attractiveness is related to their financial success, gambling losses may make some men feel less desired, and they avoid intimacy. Unfortunately, they may then believe that winning at gambling will make them attractive: "I figured the only way to get my wife interested in me again was to continue gambling until I won big. Then she would find me attractive again."

Financial

Bankruptcy, defaulting on credit cards, mortgage foreclosures, and overdue bank loan repayments are common problems among individuals with gambling disorder. Financial problems are also triggers for relapse: "I figured the only way to get out of debt was to win big." People generally do not like discussing money, and health care providers often do not ask about it. People with gambling problems need to try to talk openly with their health care professional about finances. Because so many couples' finances are intertwined, partners may suffer significant blows to their credit ratings if the gamblers do not disclose all financial problems so that they can be worked out.

Gamblers Anonymous has historically taken a negative view of bankruptcy, believing it represents another "easy out" for the gambler. Although we respect that view, we try to avoid hard and fast rules about sensitive financial matters. Financial issues within families are often complicated, and we need to think about the loved ones as well. The key point is that helping people with gambling problems should including identifying and addressing financial difficulties.

Health

The health implications of gambling are often ignored. Gamblers have high rates of health problems such as hypertension, obesity, and insomnia. Some of these problems are clearly due to time spent gambling, which can be at the expense of doing other, healthier activities, such as exercising. Some problems may be a result of the stress from gambling problems. Anyone who has a gambling problem needs a good primary care doctor and regular checkups.

Two aspects of gamblers' health, however, may not be simply consequences of gambling: nicotine dependence and obesity. Approximately 75 percent of gamblers smoke, and more than 50 percent of gamblers are overweight or obese. These two important health problems need to be addressed along with the gambling problem. Research has shown that smoking and obesity are associated with worse gambling symptoms and that smoking may make relapse to gambling more likely if not addressed. Why is that the case? One way to think about these other health issues is that they are also addictive behaviors, and they may therefore work in synergy with the gambling to make the overall addiction worse. Another explanation is that the gambler has come to associate smoking and excessive food intake with gambling. Casinos are full of large buffets, and many casinos allow patrons to smoke. Therefore, doing one activity makes the person want to do the other. We have found that having a person work on all these addictive behaviors at the same time is probably the best and healthiest option.

Mental health

In addition to physical health complications, mental health problems, particularly substance addiction, depression, and anxiety, are common among gamblers. The relationship between these mental health problems and gambling, however, is not always clear. For example, many gamblers become quite depressed and anxious about the consequences of their gambling. They cannot sleep, and they feel like failures because of their financial losses. They may drink more alcohol and develop problems with that as well. Conversely, some gamblers were depressed or anxious before they started to gamble, and the gambling is their way to "self-medicate" their uncomfortable feelings. Similarly, some people have had ongoing problems with alcohol, and their drinking leads to reckless behavior such as gambling. If possible, the physician or therapist needs to know the direction of these influences: does depression drive gambling, or does gambling lead to depression? The direction becomes important for deciding which problems should be treated first. Many people have their depression treated and wonder why they do not get better, but they have never disclosed their gambling problems, which are the driving force of their depression.

In severe cases, individuals with gambling disorder report the need for psychiatric hospitalization owing to depression and related suicidality brought on by their gambling. The often overwhelming financial consequences and guilt associated with gambling disorder may also contribute to attempted or completed suicide. Approximately 17 to 24 percent of individuals with gambling disorder report having attempted suicide because of their gambling. Why is this? For many people, financial problems from gambling have a huge ripple effect through their lives. Children's college funds are depleted, the mortgage goes unpaid, the car is repossessed, creditors are calling daily, and on and on. In addition, some people may see their finances as a reflection of their intrinsic worth. When their finances are destroyed, they feel worthless. Worse yet, they may even begin to feel like a burden to their family. Some gamblers come to feel they are worth more to their families dead than alive.

The threat of suicide can occur at any time, not just when the gambling is at its worst. Some people start getting their gambling under control and then kill themselves. Gambling debts keep popping up for months. The person may be abstinent from gambling and trying to feel better about themselves, but when the creditors call, the gambler feels hopeless. Therefore, health care providers need to ask gamblers about suicide at every visit, regardless of where in recovery the person is and how well the health care provider believes the patient is doing. The family should be informed of this risk and be diligent in taking threats of suicide very seriously by contacting mental health professionals.

Among individuals with gambling disorder and a co-occurring mental health problem, the onset of gambling disorder precedes the other mental health problem 24 percent of the time, whereas gambling follows the other mental health disorder 74 percent of the time. Mood and anxiety disorders often predict a subsequent gambling disorder, whereas it is more common for a gambling disorder to predict substance use disorders than vice versa.

How common is gambling disorder?

A range of prevalence estimates have been reported for gambling disorder depending on when the study was conducted and what instruments were used to diagnose the disorder. The first national U.S. study in 1976 noted that 0.8 percent of adults had a significant gambling problem. Twenty years later, the National Opinion Research Center conducted a national survey and found a lifetime prevalence estimate of 0.8 percent. A meta-analysis of 120 prevalence estimate surveys completed in North America from the late 1970s to the late 1990s found that the lifetime estimate of gambling disorder was 1.6 percent. Similar rates have been reported in other countries, although perhaps higher in some areas (5.3 percent in Hong Kong). A recent U.S. study, the National Epidemiologic Survey on Alcohol and Related Conditions, however, found that only 0.4 percent of adults met lifetime criteria for a gambling disorder.

So it appears that approximately 0.4 to 2.1 percent of people have a gambling disorder. To put that in perspective with other psychiatric disorders, about 0.1 percent of people have anorexia nervosa, 0.8 percent have bipolar disorder, and 2 percent have a drug addiction. So, even though the rates of gambling disorder may seem small, it is as common as or more common than many other mental health problems. The small percentage translates into millions of people worldwide. And these percentages are just for gambling *disorder*. A greater number of people would qualify for some type of gambling problem (that is, people who meet a couple of the diagnostic criteria instead of many of them). The numbers of people with this problem indicate a persistent, significant, and global public health problem.

Anyone can develop a gambling disorder. Both men and women can develop this problem, although most studies have found that gambling problems are more common in men. Women with gambling disorders, however, are more likely to seek treatment. Gambling is also a problem in all races and ethnicities. Some recent research suggests that African American individuals may be three times more likely to have a gambling problem than Caucasian individuals.

Gambling disorder is also more common among people who already have some mental health issues. For example, among people who are in treatment for drug or alcohol addiction, gambling disorder prevalence ranges from 5 to 33 percent. Among people with general mental health issues, the prevalence of gambling disorder has ranged from 4.9 percent in adolescents to 6.9 percent in adults.

There has been a proliferation, and an accelerated proliferation, of gambling venues during the past decade, particularly with online gaming, Native American casinos, riverboat gambling, and significant expansions in Asiatic countries (Macau, for example). With increased opportunity to gamble, more people are likely to develop gambling disorder in the future.

Does gambling disorder differ based on age, gender, and culture?

Gender

Significant differences have been observed in men and women with gambling disorder. Men with gambling disorder are more likely to be single, live alone, have sought treatment for substance abuse, have higher rates of antisocial personality traits, and have marital consequences related to their gambling. Though men seem to start gambling at earlier ages and have higher rates of gambling disorder, women tend to start gambling later in life but have a shorter period between starting their gambling and developing a problem (the telescoping phenomenon mentioned earlier). Women with gambling disorder are also more likely to seek treatment for and recover from their gambling problems.

Men prefer different types of gambling than women do. Men with gambling disorder have higher rates of "strategic" forms of gambling, including sports betting, video poker, and blackjack. They often say they want to be like James Bond and to have people notice and admire them: "I felt sexy winning at blackjack. I thought every woman wanted me at that moment and that every man wanted to be me." Men enjoy the thrill of gambling, the risky quality of it, and they feel powerful when they win. Women, on the other hand, have higher rates of "nonstrategic" gambling, such as slot machines or bingo. Women describe gambling as a way of escaping life issues and getting away from responsibilities and stress. Contrary to many men with gambling disorder, women do not typically want to be noticed when they gamble.

Age

Gambling disorder is more common among younger and middle-aged persons than among older adults. Among adolescents and young adults, the disorder is more prevalent in males. Younger individuals prefer different forms of gambling (for example, sports betting), while older adults are more likely to develop problems with slot machine and bingo gambling. Although the proportions of individuals who seek treatment for gambling disorder are low across all age groups, younger individuals are the least likely to seek treatment. This is a real concern, because by the time most people come for treatment, they have had the problem for many years. A problem like gambling is much easier to treat when caught in the early years of the illness than when someone has been gambling for many years. Gambling disorder can be successfully treated, however, no matter how long the person has been gambling.

Culture

People from different cultures and different races or ethnicities are more likely to participate in certain types of gambling activities.

Is a problem with gambling always a gambling disorder?

Gambling "too much" does not necessarily mean a person has a gambling disorder. Not all gambling equals a gambling disorder. If someone goes to Las Vegas with friends once a year and each time gambles a bit more than he should, would we want to diagnose that behavior as a gambling disorder? No. Gambling disorder must be distinguished from recreational or professional gambling. Recreational gambling is when friends or colleagues get together for a limited time and suffer acceptable losses. In professional gambling, where the person is making a living by gambling, risks are limited.

In neither recreational nor professional gambling does the person have a gambling disorder. But it can be difficult to judge whether the gambling is truly recreational or professional. Consider the person who is losing a lot at gambling but claims to be working toward becoming a professional gambler. "I think my losses are acceptable, because I'm honing my gambling skills. My family thinks I have a problem, but they don't understand my goals." Is the person simply in denial about her gambling? Or is it possible that she is making efforts to become a professional, such as reading about gambling and studying other professionals, and in fact may not have a problem? This is where the diagnostic criteria listed above can be very useful.

Excessive gambling may also occur when people struggle with their mood. For example, gambling may occur during a manic episode. A manic episode is a mood disorder in which a person is out of control, feeling too euphoric (or extremely irritable), and engaging in multiple impulsive behaviors that are getting him into trouble. A manic episode is the defining feature of bipolar disorder (also sometimes referred to as manic depressive illness). Gambling may be one of these impulsive behaviors. If the problematic gambling behavior also occurs when the person's mood is stable, the individual may have gambling disorder in addition to bipolar disorder. An individual with gambling disorder may, during a period of gambling, exhibit behavior that resembles a manic episode (for example, feeling euphoric, not sleeping, acting impulsively). When these symptoms occur only during a gambling episode, then the person would not meet criteria for bipolar disorder. This distinction is important, because the treatment for bipolar disorder is very different from the treatment for gambling disorder.

As we mentioned earlier, excessive gambling can occur when a person is intoxicated with alcohol or high on drugs. The person may act impulsively and wager irresponsibly. If the gambling does not occur when the person is sober, then the appropriate diagnosis may be a substance use disorder.

Finally, it is important to find out whether the person started gambling after beginning any medications. Some patients taking certain medications (for example, medications to treat Parkinson's disease or restless leg syndrome, or aripiprazole for depression or psychosis) may experience urges to gamble and may act on those urges. These medications may increase dopamine in a specific part of the brain that controls our urges or need for rewarding stimulation. If gambling behavior decreases or stops when the medication is reduced in dosage or is discontinued, then a primary diagnosis of gambling disorder would not be warranted, because the symptoms were a direct consequence of medication.

Are gambling disorders genetic?

Mental health problems affect many first-degree relatives of people with a gambling disorder. In two studies of first-degree relatives of gamblers, 17 to 33 percent had a mood disorder, and 18 to 24 percent reported an alcohol problem. Other studies have found that 20 percent of first-degree relatives of those with a gambling disorder also have a gambling disorder. In fact, individuals with a problem gambling parent had a 3.3 times higher risk of having a gambling disorder compared with the background population.

Research using the Vietnam Era Twin Registry (male adults) found that 12 to 20 percent of genetic and 3 to 8 percent of nonshared environmental variation in risk for gambling disorder was accounted for by risk of alcoholism. Data from the national Australian Twin Registry found that up to two-thirds of the association between alcoholism and gambling disorder was attributable to shared genetic vulnerability.

What do all of these data mean? Simply put, gambling appears to run in families with other addictions and appears to have a genetic link to alcoholism. Alcoholism in a family appears to make a person more vulnerable to developing not only an alcohol problem but also a gambling problem. Genetic influences are only a *potential* problem, however. Having a family member with a gambling disorder does not automatically mean that someone in the family will develop such a problem. Perhaps most important, genetics do not seem to have any major influence on whether someone can be successfully treated for gambling. One man who had read the literature on the genetics of gambling asked, "So, if this is genetics, I can't do anything about it, right?" Genetics does not mean that the person cannot or should not take responsibility for the behavior, and it does not mean the person cannot get better.

The gambling brain

Although no one yet knows the cause of gambling disorder, we do know that various chemicals in the brain may contribute to the behavior. Why one person has a chemical imbalance and another does not is still unknown. The imbalance could be due to genetics, developmental issues, life events, or some unknown reason. Having said that, we do know that multiple neurotransmitter systems (for example, dopaminergic, glutamatergic, serotonergic, noradrenergic, opioidergic) are involved in the development of gambling disorder.

Dopamine is involved in learning, motivation, and the importance of stimuli, including rewards. Alterations in dopaminergic pathways have been proposed as an underlying reason for seeking rewards (for example, through gambling) that trigger the release of dopamine and produce feelings of pleasure. Contrary to what might be expected from dopamine involvement, drugs that block dopamine (for example, olanzapine) do not seem to help in the treatment of gambling disorder.

A strong body of evidence based on twenty years of animal research suggests that the neurochemical glutamate is critical in drug reward, reinforcement, and relapse. Some data from cerebrospinal fluid studies (the fluid that bathes the brain) also suggest that a dysfunctional glutamate system is a factor in gambling disorder. As we discuss elsewhere, this may be why a nutritional supplement such as N-acetylcysteine has shown some promise in treating gambling problems.

Serotonin may also play a role in gambling disorder. For example, when animals are given too much serotonin, they are not able to judge between expected outcomes based on the relative likelihood and size of rewards and punishments. In humans, research on people with gambling disorders has shown decreased levels of platelet monoamine oxidase B (MAO-B) (a peripheral marker of serotonergic function) and low levels of serotonin metabolites (5-HIAA) in cerebrospinal fluid. Both findings may suggest that people with gambling disorder have some sort of serotonin deficiency.

The noradrenergic system (centrally involved in the "fight or flight" response) has also been examined for its possible associations with gambling disorder. Studies have found that individuals with gambling disorder have significantly higher cerebrospinal fluid levels of a main metabolite of the noradrenergic system. In addition, individuals with gambling disorder appear to maintain higher noradrenergic levels during an entire gambling session, whereas healthy control gamblers (without the disorder) exhibit elevated levels only at the start of the gambling session.

Finally, the endogenous opioid system, which influences the experience of pleasure, has been implicated in gambling disorder. Opioids also modify dopamine in the brain. Gambling has been associated with elevated blood levels of endorphins, and opioid receptor antagonists (see below, in treatment) have shown significant promise in the treatment of gambling disorder.

Psychological factors

The behaviors that characterize gambling disorder (for example, chasing losses, preoccupation with gambling, inability to stop) are suggestive of underlying problems with cognitive functions. Such behaviors are impulsive because they are often premature, poorly thought out, risky, and likely to result in negative long-term outcomes. Impulsive behavior underlying gambling disorder tends to begin during late adolescence or early adulthood. Deficits across multiple cognitive functions have been found in people with gambling disorder, including aspects of inhibition, working memory, planning, cognitive flexibility, and time management.

No clear link has been established between the severity of cognitive deficits and the severity of clinically significant symptoms, however. These cognitive problems may occur in people at risk before symptoms develop, or they may stem from the disorder itself. Most likely, some cognitive deficits make a person more likely to develop a gambling disorder (perhaps with a given cognitive problem even running in families). Findings from people at risk of gambling disorder suggest that deficits in decision making are evident before the illness develops. Other cognitive difficulties, however, could be a consequence of recurrent gambling itself.

Social and environmental factors

Multiple environmental factors may also contribute to developmental pathways of gambling disorder. The structural and situational characteristics of gambling activities (for example, accessibility to gambling, exposure to gambling, location and type of gambling establishment, size and number of prizes) can all play a role in the development and persistence of gambling behaviors.

Rates of early negative childhood experiences, such as abuse and trauma, appear to be higher among individuals with gambling disorder relative to recreational gamblers. The severity of maltreatment is associated with the severity of gambling problems and an earlier age of onset of gambling. Because trauma has been associated with lower quality of life and self-esteem as well as substance addictions, it may indirectly affect gambling behavior.

How is gambling disorder treated?

Despite the significant personal costs associated with gambling disorder, only a small proportion, around 6 percent, of those suffering from gambling disorder seek proper treatment. A desire to handle the problem on their own, lack of information about where to receive treatment, and feelings of shame make people less willing to seek treatment. Treatment for gambling can largely be grouped under three headings: psychotherapy, Gamblers Anonymous, and medication. We discuss each of these approaches below.

What happens if the person does not receive treatment?

Gambling disorder often begins in adolescence or early adulthood but can start during middle age or even older adulthood. Generally, gambling disorder develops over the course of years. Most individuals who develop a gambling disorder show a pattern of gambling that gradually increases in both frequency and amount of wagering. Gambling patterns may be regular or episodic, and gambling disorder can be persistent or can come and go. Gambling may increase during periods of stress or depression.

Approximately 30 percent of individuals with gambling disorder experience natural recovery, without undergoing formal treatment or attending Gamblers Anonymous. Although it is possible that someone will simply stop gambling if they do not receive treatment, the majority of individuals with gambling disorder—70 percent—will not improve on their own. This fact underscores the need for evidence-based treatments.

Treatment goals

There are several goals when someone begins treatment for gambling disorder. First, the person should be clear about what he or she expects from treatment. Some patients may wish to stop gambling, while others may want to develop more control over their behavior. For many people, *harm reduction*, instead of total abstinence, may be a reasonable and achievable goal. Consequently, individuals may want to work with a physician or therapist who offers multiple goals (such as abstinence, decreased gambling, more control) to individuals with a gambling disorder. The problem is that there are no data to suggest, on an individual level, which people should remain abstinent compared to which should aim instead to reduce but not completely stop their behavior.

Second, people with gambling problems often want to know which treatment is best. There are, however, no comparison studies of the various treatment approaches, and so there is little evidence-based guidance for choosing a treatment goal. This means that the person needs to feel comfortable with the physician or therapist, so that he or she is able to discuss changing the treatment approach if the first one does not work.

People who have a gambling disorder exhibit high rates of placebo response in treatment studies. A placebo response does not mean that there is something psychologically wrong with the person or that all treatments are equally good. Instead, it probably reflects the fact that many approaches, including just talking about gambling for the first time, produce benefit in the short term. This initial robust response, however, may cause many people to drop out of treatment prematurely, feeling that the problem is controlled. Individuals should therefore understand that although many approaches may help substantially at first, it is important to continue with treatments as long as their clinician recommends them.

Many impulsive patients do not follow treatment recommendations or follow up with treatment. Therefore, a treatment goal is to *stay in treatment* until the *improvement is lasting*. Patients often believe that they are doing better than in fact they are, and therefore they see treatment as unnecessary; or they do not have an instantaneous response, and therefore they do not stay with treatment. Both of these concerns can be minimized by involving a family member or close friend in treatment to assist the patient in monitoring behavior, to provide accountability, and to provide a realistic view of the patient's behavior and of treatment.

Which type of psychotherapy is best for gambling disorder?

Although a variety of psychotherapy treatments have been examined, advertised, and talked about on the Internet, only a few have evidence to support their use. Of course, we know of people with gambling problems who have done well with all sorts of treatments; however, unless evidence demonstrates the usefulness of a particular treatment, there is simply no way to ethically recommend it. Therefore, we present the treatments that we know work based on evidence from the scientific literature.

Cognitive behavioral therapy

The most studied psychotherapies for gambling disorder are probably cognitive and behavioral approaches. These therapies are usually used together. Behavioral approaches focus on developing alternate activities to compete with gambling-specific reinforcers as well as identifying gambling triggers. For example, if the person usually gambles on Friday night because she is bored or lonely, then she might schedule some other exciting activity to do with friends on Friday nights.

Cognitive strategies have traditionally included changing the way a person thinks about gambling, the triggers that lead to gambling, and the consequences of gambling. Any number of thoughts can be distorted when gambling is involved. For example, the gambler believes that he can control the outcomes of games based on which socks he is wearing. He may also believe that the only way to cope with stress is by gambling. Another thought might be that gambling and winning will bring new life into his marriage. Gamblers may also think in absolute black and white terms—either they win and are somebody of worth or they lose and nobody thinks well of them. Through therapy, all these thoughts can be modified, and the person can learn new ways of thinking.

Is this the same as positive affirmations?

No. Cognitive therapy does not tell the person that everything is wonderful or that she is a terrific person. It makes the person "look at the evidence" and think through her triggers, feelings, or how she see gambling based on this evidence. An example might be to have the person make the logical connections between socks and gambling outcomes: "What evidence do you have that your socks are lucky?"

Cognitive behavioral therapy takes a lot of work on the part of the patient. There is usually a daily diary of thoughts to record, and perhaps some other homework assignments. Homework is a large part of the therapy. Gamblers need to change their way of thinking, and that takes time and practice. We tell patients that therapy is like practicing the piano. No one learns how to do it unless they practice between lessons. Cognitive behavioral therapy takes daily practice. Nothing the therapist says is suddenly going to stop the person from gambling. For gamblers who often want things quickly, therapy can be difficult.

How long does a person do this therapy?

In most cases, therapy sessions are once a week, last for sixty minutes each session, and usually continue for about four months. After that period, the person may return every couple of months for another eight months or so for "booster" sessions of therapy, which focus on the cognitive and behavioral techniques the person has previously learned.

Some people can do equally well with less therapy. Brief treatments (for example, using a self-help cognitive behavioral therapy workbook) have shown benefit for people with gambling disorder. Some of these treatments may be only a single session of therapy, or a few sessions. Brief versions of therapy may be best for people with a milder form of gambling disorder, or those who would struggle to attend longer-term treatment programs.

What if the person does not want therapy?

Ambivalence about treatment is common with gamblers. This may be because the person loves gambling and simply does not want to stop. Many gamblers want to stop losing but do not want to stop gambling. Gamblers also may want to stop right after losing a large amount, but when they calm down and realize that the world did not end, they may not want to stop. Their perspective can change overnight.

Motivational interviewing is a technique that assumes that ambivalence is a primary obstacle to change. Having individuals describe and listen to their own statements about changing behavior can reduce their ambivalence and strengthen their commitment to change. Motivational interviewing is empathic and uses the strengths of the gambler to enhance self-efficacy regarding changes in behavior. It is often used in combination with cognitive behavioral therapy or on its own as a brief individual intervention. It can also be used in a group format.

Should a gambler avoid the triggers to gamble?

Cue exposure, based on conditioning theory, is a well-validated form of cognitive behavioral therapy used in the treatment of fear-based problems. The goal is to extinguish a learned response through repeated exposure to a conditioned stimulus in the absence of the consequence. For example, a person who is afraid of entrusting a document to the postal service might be asked to mail materials to himself every day for several weeks, with the outcome of receiving the materials through the postal service.

There is evidence that cue reactivity to relevant triggers is an important factor in relapse to gambling disorder, particularly in the context of negative mood. For example, when the gambler is upset after a long day at work, the sight of the casino billboard results in an intense urge to gamble. *Imaginal desensitization,* a type of therapy, involves an imagination exercise in which the person thinks of the triggers (that is, the place, feelings, and thoughts) that generate an urge to gamble. The exercise then takes the person through a typical gambling episode, induces the negative consequences as well, and then ends with the person taking control of the situation and not gambling. By going through these exercises multiple times each day, the person learns how to deal with a range of triggers.

Should a gambler use individual therapy or group therapy?

Both individual and group therapy have shown benefit for gambling disorder. If choosing group therapy, however, it is important to realize that the only type of group therapy with evidence for helping gambling disorder is group cognitive behavioral therapy. A typical support group has no robust published evidence for being effective in treating gambling disorder.

When should a gambler go to residential treatment?

There are really little, if any, data for the use of residential treatment for gambling. When someone cannot gain any control over his or her gambling by using outpatient individual therapy, however, residential treatment may be useful. Having treated thousands of gamblers over the years, we have found that only a handful of people have ever truly needed residential programs.

Gamblers Anonymous

Another type of treatment is Gamblers Anonymous (GA), a self-help group currently operating in at least fifty-five countries worldwide. Individuals use a program of twelve steps and twelve traditions, modified from Alcoholics Anonymous, to acknowledge powerlessness over compulsive gambling and to remain gambling-free. The groups promote a sense of common purpose and understanding as well as reinforcement of each consecutive day of abstinence from gambling. Although there are not a lot of data for GA, many people swear by it, and there is no reason it could not be used in combination with other treatment options.

Are medications useful for gambling disorder?

Although no medication has received regulatory approval as a treatment for gambling disorder, various pharmacological agents (opioid antagonists, glutamatergic agents, antidepressants, lithium) have demonstrated benefit in treating gambling addiction. For someone with a gambling disorder, medications are often useful, but they are not "magic pills." Given the impulsivity of many gamblers and the desire for an "easy fix" to their problems, the option of medication needs to come with a lot of education around expectations. In addition, the person has to commit to taking the medication consistently, as prescribed.

The medication that has shown the best and most consistent benefit for gambling disorder is naltrexone, an opioid antagonist approved by the FDA for the treatment of alcoholism and opiate addiction. Naltrexone appears to be beneficial because it reduces the intensity of urges to gamble, gambling thoughts, and gambling behavior. Naltrexone may be even more beneficial for gamblers who have a positive family history of moderate to severe alcohol problems. Beneficial dosing of naltrexone ranges from 50 mg per day to 150 mg per day. The FDA has issued a warning of liver problems with doses over 50 mg per day.

People should be aware of possible side effects associated with naltrexone. The most common side effect is nausea, so the medication should be taken after eating food. The nausea is likely to diminish if a person stays on treatment for more than a couple of days. The more serious side effect is that naltrexone can cause irritation to the liver. This is not common but can occur, and if the irritation is significant, the medication should be stopped. The chance of liver involvement can be reduced by eliminating the use of over-the-counter nonsteroidal analgesics (NSAIDs, or nonsteroidal anti-inflammatory drugs, such as ibuprofen, aspirin, naproxen, and others), as they tend to increase the chance of liver irritation.

Because there is evidence that chemical dysfunction in the brain's reward system (particularly a chemical called glutamate) may result in unhealthy reward-seeking behavior, N-acetylcysteine (NAC), an amino acid and glutamate-modulating agent, has been investigated as a treatment for gambling disorder. NAC is sold as an over-the-counter nutritional supplement that is regarded as an antioxidant generally good for the liver and the immune system. NAC can significantly decrease urges and gambling behavior in individuals with gambling disorder. Dosing for NAC generally starts at 600 mg twice a day and then goes up to 1200 mg twice a day. The most common side effect can be some mild nausea or flatulence, but otherwise the medication is usually very well tolerated.

Trials of serotonergic antidepressants have produced mixed results for gambling disorder but are likely to be more useful when low mood or clinical depression is also present. The atypical antipsychotic, olanzapine, demonstrated negative results, and a trial of bupropion failed to demonstrate any benefit over placebo. Lithium has shown a benefit for gamblers who have features of bipolar disorder, such as symptoms of mania.

Based on all the published research, naltrexone appears to be the most promising medication for gambling disorder. Because not everyone will benefit from naltrexone, other options are needed. In those cases, NAC or lithium could be viable alternatives.

How long does a person have to take medication?

If someone has found a medication helpful, we recommend that the person stay on the medication for at least one year. If the person's symptoms worsen after stopping the medication, it can be restarted and again given for another year.

Can a person receive therapy and medication together?

Yes. In fact, in our clinic we find that this combination produces the best results for most people, and research supports the combination of medication with therapy. No data suggest that using therapy and medication together would reduce the effectiveness of either treatment.

What if therapy does not work?

Because most people who seek treatment for gambling disorder are provided with individual therapy, several strategies are available when therapy does not work. First, the individual should be offered a course of medication (naltrexone, NAC, or lithium) as part of treatment. Second, for those who have not responded to standard individual cognitive behavioral therapy, adding imaginal desensitization, motivational interviewing, group therapy, or GA may be beneficial. Third, the person may need to be reassessed for other mental health issues, because these other conditions (for example, alcohol or substance use, bipolar disorder, use of dopaminergic medications) may be preventing the person from responding to standard treatment approaches.

Special issues in treatment

Several common situations may influence which treatment approach is best for a particular individual who has gambling disorder.

1. If there is active substance use, the question is whether the person can be treated as an outpatient and the same approach

used to treat the substance addiction and the gambling disorder. If the substance use interferes with gambling treatment, the individual may need to be referred for detoxification or residential placement for the drug addiction before receiving the gambling-focused therapy.

2. When an individual with gambling disorder also exhibits clear signs of mania, this symptom needs to be addressed. The mania will need to be treated before the person can take full advantage of the treatment for gambling disorder. In most cases, treatment for mania will involve medication to stabilize the person's mood.

3. When individuals with gambling disorder have significant personality disorders, such as borderline personality disorder, the standard treatment plan for gambling disorder may need to be modified. Adding dialectical behavior therapy (DBT) elements to standard treatment may be beneficial, or the person may need to be referred for DBT, which can be done simultaneously with the gambling treatment.

4. Many female gamblers report a history of trauma. The rates of trauma in these patients are significantly higher than the rates in the population at large. The person with gambling disorder and trauma history may benefit from therapy directly focusing on the trauma. There are no data to guide us as to whether the trauma therapy should come first, should take place simultaneously with gambling therapy, or wait until the gambling is under control. In most cases, because of the seriousness of both problems, we suggest that the therapies be done simultaneously.

5. Given the high rates of suicide and suicide attempts among individuals with gambling disorder, the physician or therapist needs to assess for suicidal thinking or intentions at each visit. When people become suicidal and are a threat to themselves, the treatment for gambling will need to be interrupted, and the focus should be on safety and suicide prevention. Inpatient hospitalization may be necessary.

Case

Michael is a 33-year-old married man with a full-time job. He has a limited psychiatric history but acknowledges a history of alcohol abuse in his early twenties and reports having been sober for the past ten years. Michael reports that stress at work has recently increased. When times became stressful at work years ago, he used to have "a beer or two" to calm his nerves. Now free from alcohol use, Michael tries to exercise after work to relieve stress, but he usually cannot find the time. After a particularly stressful week of work, Michael sees a billboard for a casino nearby and decides to go. He wins playing blackjack, and the next week he finds himself thinking about gambling and decides to go to the casino again. This time he loses, but because he believes this is just "bad luck," he decides to leave work early on the false pretense of a doctor's appointment to go to the casino again midweek. Over the next few weeks, Michael's gambling increases to about three times a week, and the losses start to add up. He begins lying to his wife, saying that he has been loaning money to a friend and helping his friend with a new business.

When he comes to the clinic, Michael is screened for gambling disorder, and his symptoms meet seven of the nine *DSM-5* criteria listed, indicating that he has a "moderate" gambling disorder. When assessing the available treatment options for Michael, two elements of his gambling and mental health history suggest that appropriate treatment is a combination of medication and therapy. First, he has a personal and family history of alcohol abuse. Research has shown that individuals with gambling disorder and a family history of alcoholism respond well to opioid antagonists such as naltrexone. In addition, the intense urges to gamble, which Michael acknowledges having, are targeted by this class of medication. Second, he reports cognitive distortions (for example, feeling that he can control his luck), which respond to cognitive therapies. Further, given the social isolation that gambling has caused, he is given a list of locations of GA meetings to build a supportive network.

Key Points for Individuals with Gambling Disorder

1. Gambling disorder is a real mental health problem with effective treatment options.
2. Gamblers should try their best to be open and honest with their physician or therapist about the behavior and its effects on finances, relationships, and other aspects of life. It is only through being aware of the full impact of the problem that a clinician can ensure an individual gets optimal treatment.
3. Gambling disorder appears to run in families with other addictions, but that does not mean you cannot learn to control the behavior.
4. You need to work with your family and other loved ones to get better. This may mean turning over control of finances for a period, allowing loved ones to take you to appointments and help with therapy homework, and working with your family to develop healthy replacement behaviors.

Key Points for Family Members

1. The diagnosis and treatment of a gambling disorder needs to be taken seriously.
2. Family members should consider—with the person's permission—taking control of credit cards, checkbooks, and salaries until the person has the gambling under control.
3. Family members may need to meet with their own financial adviser to see how best to preserve their financial health.
4. The gambler may do well at first, but family need to be cautious in thinking that this rapid response to therapy means the problem is solved.
5. Because of the trust issues that gambling creates within families, family members may need their own counseling. In addition, many family members find support through Gam-Anon meetings.

4

Stealing

Janice started shoplifting in high school. At first she stole some inexpensive items on a dare. Not only did she not get into any trouble with the behavior, she discovered that she liked the feeling it created inside her—she felt powerful and nearly euphoric. She continued to steal during her time in college and while studying for her master's degree in business. She was arrested once but was freed with no repercussions after fabricating a story about how the item simply fell into her purse. Now 45 years old, Janice is married and has two adolescent children.

Janice sought treatment for the behavior after so many years because her husband threatened to divorce her over the stealing. She had told him about the stealing a few years before she came for treatment, leaving out many details and downplaying how often she stole and how intensely she felt the desire to steal. Her husband felt that her behavior could jeopardize his career and the futures of their children.

Although Janice certainly could have paid for the items she stole, she had continued to steal something at least once a week for years. The items she stole increased in price over time, as she began stealing cashmere scarves and nice leather products. The riskiness of her thefts also increased as she stole from stores that she knew were fairly well monitored by security. She described these acts as driven by thrill seeking.

Janice's weekly therapy was started using a cognitive behavioral approach, with motivational interviewing to address the ambivalence as well as imaginal exposure exercises to help Janice cope with her urges to steal when in stores. In addition, she was started on off-label naltrexone, 50 mg per day, to reduce her urges to steal. Janice responded well to therapy and medication, and by week four of treatment, she reported that she was no longer stealing. The therapy was continued weekly for ten weeks, and then once a month for the next year.

Why should we be concerned about people who steal?

Stealing is a common behavior. Although the exact prevalence of shoplifting is unknown (because many who steal are never caught), approximately 10 percent of randomly chosen customers followed while shopping have been observed stealing. It is estimated that more than $10 billion worth of goods are stolen from retailers each year, which translates into more than $25 million each day. Most shoplifters are described as amateurs with sporadic activity and no known criminal history, who steal for their own consumption rather than for resale. Studies involving apprehended shoplifters indicate that shoplifting may be more common in women than in men. The higher rates of women among people seeking help for shoplifting may be falsely elevated because women may be more likely referred for mental health evaluation than men. Male shoplifters are more likely to be apprehended during adolescence and early adulthood, whereas women are more likely to be apprehended during puberty or early adulthood and around the age of menopause. Some of these same studies also revealed that shoplifting was not related to lower socioeconomic level and that most people stole for personal gain.

The vast majority of people who steal would not qualify for a mental health diagnosis. A minority of these individuals, however, may be unable to control their behavior and may benefit from treatment. These people would likely receive the diagnosis of *kleptomania*. Kleptomania is characterized by repetitive stealing behavior brought on by significant and uncontrollable urges to steal items. Kleptomania is associated with significant psychosocial and legal consequences as well as elevated risk for suicide. Individuals with kleptomania differ from "ordinary" shoplifters in that they have urges to steal things and feel they are not able to stop their behavior. Fewer than 5 percent of all shoplifters have kleptomania.

This form of stealing, kleptomania, has been defined as a mental health problem by the American Psychiatric Association, in their fifth edition of the *Diagnostic and Statistical Manual of Mental Disorders* (DSM-5). The idea of stealing becoming a problem for some people is not a new one. In fact, an inability to stop oneself from stealing has been recognized for at least one hundred years by the medical community.

How is kleptomania diagnosed?

Like all mental health disorders, kleptomania has no blood test for determining whether someone has the disorder. Although research has identified certain distinct findings on brain scans in people with kleptomania, there is also no way to determine whether someone has this disorder simply by performing a brain scan. At this time, the diagnosis is made by what a person tells her health care provider.

People with kleptomania tend to be very secretive about their stealing, and family members often do not know anything about the behavior. Most people never tell their partners or friends about their behavior, most likely due to shame. Even the information the clinician receives from the person who has the disorder is likely to be incomplete, particularly at first. People may falsely assume that if they tell a health care provider about stealing, the clinician will report them to the police. We have treated some individuals for years before they felt comfortable disclosing their entire stealing history. Trust may take time to develop.

The essential feature of kleptomania is persistent and recurrent stealing that results in psychosocial dysfunction. To receive the diagnosis of kleptomania, an individual must exhibit all of the following:

1. Recurrent failure to resist impulses to steal objects that are not needed for personal use or for their monetary value. This criterion

is simply to separate people with kleptomania from ordinary thieves. The problem is that behaviors are complex. Many of our patients over the years have reported that although stealing is what they enjoy, if they can also get something useful, then why not? The "personal use" element of this criterion is therefore probably overly restrictive.

2. Increasing sense of tension immediately before committing the theft. This criterion reflects the buildup of impulsivity in people with kleptomania. The problem with this criterion is that the illness probably changes over time. Many of our patients who have been stealing for decades no longer report a buildup of tension. In fact, they steal often because they anticipate that tension will develop, and they want to avoid the tension.

3. Pleasure, gratification, or relief at the time of committing the theft; this criterion seems to be appropriate for the majority of people with kleptomania.

4. Absence of other motivations for the stealing. The theft is not committed to express anger or vengeance and is not done in response to a delusion or a hallucination; the stealing is not better accounted for by conduct disorder, a manic episode, or antisocial personality disorder. These criteria make a distinction between someone who has kleptomania and someone who is stealing because of other mental health problems, such as a personality disorder, bipolar disorder, or schizophrenia; all of these disorders would require different types of treatment.

How is this diagnosis made accurately? We think the key is in the first criterion—kleptomania is a problem when people cannot control the behavior. We believe it less important to focus on what is stolen than on the loss of control. Criminals can control their behavior, but kleptomaniacs cannot. Furthermore, in kleptomania, the objects stolen are usually of little value and are affordable to the individual, who will then typically discard, hoard, secretly return them, or give them away. Individuals may avoid stealing when immediate arrest is likely, but the chances of apprehension are usually not fully taken into account. In kleptomania, the impulse to steal is experienced as wrong, senseless, and incompatible with the individual's self-concept. Although a sense of pleasure, gratification, or relief is experienced at the time of the theft, individuals describe a feeling of guilt, remorse, or depression soon (if not immediately) afterward.

Clinical aspects of kleptomania

The average age at onset of stealing behavior is during adolescence, although reports of new onset stealing behaviors occur as early as 4 years old and as late as 77 years. The mean age at time of evaluation is typically mid-thirties to late thirties. Women usually present for evaluation at a younger age than men—perhaps at about 35 years of age compared to 50 years of age for men. The length of time between age of onset and age at evaluation reinforces the guilt, shame, and secrecy involved in this disorder. Among all the studies that have examined people seeking treatment for kleptomania, the rates of marriage range from 35 to 83 percent, and an education level of at least some university was true for between 19 and 100 percent. One study found that most of the patients were in the middle to lower economic brackets.

Three courses of this illness have been described: sporadic, with brief episodes and long periods of remission; episodic, with protracted periods of stealing and periods of remission; and chronic, with some degree of fluctuation. Most patients report sudden onset with a chronic course. One study of individuals with kleptomania revealed that they stole, on average, two times a week and had urges three to four days a week. Approximately one-fifth reported never having a day without symptoms, and no one went longer than three weeks without stealing.

Of those people with kleptomania who were apprehended, 79 percent reported that urges to steal were virtually abolished, but only for an average of three to four days. Subjects reported that they stole mainly from stores. All stated that they could afford what they stole and did not understand why they stole. Most reported that the value of stolen items increased over time and that most items were kept (or hoarded), although many were given away, returned, or discarded. Examples of commonly stolen objects include sweets, newspapers, food, books, and clothes.

Can this disorder be diagnosed in children?

Both typical shoplifting and kleptomania may start at a relatively early age. Young children generally have little, if any, concept of stealing—for them, desiring or wanting the object means possessing the object. By the age of 6 or 7, children begin to realize they are doing something wrong when they take something that doesn't belong to them. Children may steal because they are unhappy, lonely, jealous, fearful, or craving attention. For older children and adolescents, stealing can be used to gain acceptance by a group, but it is also a strong predictor of future delinquency and is sometimes a marker for families lacking in warmth and personal stimulation. A strong attachment to parents decreases involvement in shoplifting.

Overall, studies have shown that roughly 40 percent of apprehended shoplifters are adolescents, with most stealing peaking around the tenth grade and then declining. Possible reasons for the high rates of adolescent theft are that it is an immature response to the stressful transition to adulthood, to an inability to purchase certain items, and to increased opportunity. The steepest gain in independence occurs around age 16, when most adolescents are allowed to drive and work. On the other hand, adolescents report that they shoplift because of the novelty and risk involved, social reasons, and desire for the product. How many of these adolescent shoplifters currently suffer from, or will develop, a problem with kleptomania is not clear.

The age of onset of kleptomania appears to be most often late adolescence, yet there is little information on how this behavior occurs among and affects adolescents. There is some evidence that the current diagnostic criteria apply to adolescents who report being unable to control their shoplifting.

Consequences of kleptomania

Most individuals with kleptomania try unsuccessfully to stop stealing. The inability to stop causes feelings of shame and guilt and often leads to arrest: the majority of people with kleptomania have been apprehended at some time because of their stealing behavior. Perhaps not surprisingly, kleptomania is associated with high rates of depression, anxiety, and substance addiction. Suicidal attempts are, unfortunately, common.

Individuals with kleptomania try various ways of controlling their behavior: not leaving the house, shopping with friends and family, shopping when stores are busy, and thinking about getting caught. The majority (77.3 percent) experience guilt and shame, with 27.3 percent reporting psychiatric hospitalization, and 18.2 percent considering suicide because of their behavior. Only 41.7 percent told their spouses; the rest did not because of the shame and guilt they felt.

The criminal consequences of kleptomania seem clear. One study found that 77.5 percent of individuals with kleptomania had been arrested for shoplifting and 17.5 percent served jail time.

Interpersonal relationships, work productivity, and general well-being are all affected by kleptomania. Nearly all (97.5 percent) people with the disorder actively lied to loved ones about their behavior, and 47.5 percent felt their stealing directly led to the deterioration of these relationships. Almost half reported significant work impairment through time wasted dealing with urges, guilt, and the personal or legal consequences of their behavior. Those who suffer from kleptomania also report high levels of perceived stress (finding their lives to be unpredictable, uncontrollable, and stressful), which appears to be associated with the severity of kleptomania symptoms. People with kleptomania also have a significantly poorer quality of life compared with the general population.

Courts can be very hard on people with kleptomania, and many people in the legal community believe that kleptomania is an excuse for criminal behavior. Little is known about how much kleptomania contributes to economic losses, so most of the figures are extrapolated from shoplifting data. The incidence of shoplifting has substantially increased in the past forty years, partly because of the increase in supermarket and display merchandising. Some suggest that kleptomania is a consequence of consumerism and the abundance of commodities in modern society. In 2013, there were an estimated 27 million shoplifters (1 of every 11 people) in the United States, resulting in more than $13 billion in annual losses. If the prevalence of kleptomania is truly 6 of every 1,000 persons, then there are approximately 1.4 million individuals with kleptomania in the United States alone. Shoplifting results in increased prices to cover anticipated losses, as well as delays and intrusions from locks, tags, and surveillance.

Associated mental health problems: cause or effect?

High rates of other mental health problems have been found in patients with kleptomania. *Comorbidity* is the word used to describe having more than one medical problem. Rates of lifetime comorbid mood disorders range from 59 to 100 percent, with lifetime comorbid bipolar disorder ranging from 9 to 27 percent. High lifetime rates of comorbid anxiety disorders (60 to 80 percent), impulse control disorders (20 to 46 percent), substance addictions (23 to 50 percent), and eating disorders (60 percent) have also been reported.

Various explanations for these comorbidities have been proposed. Some have suggested that kleptomania is impulsive, and many of these other disorders are impulsive as well. Therefore, perhaps stealing is simply one aspect of being impulsive. The behaviors that characterize kleptomania (for example, urges to steal, inability to stop) are frequently poorly thought out, risky, and result in deleterious long-term outcomes. Psychological testing has demonstrated greater impulsivity, problems controlling one's behavior, and a greater need for sensation-seeking activities among individuals with kleptomania compared to controls (those without kleptomania). One study comparing the brain scans of individuals with kleptomania to healthy controls found that the part of the brain that helps us say "no" to desire may have some deficiencies.

Many people have suggested that kleptomania is merely a symptom of an antisocial or borderline personality disorder. This does not appear to be the case. In fact, rates of personality disorders among people with kleptomania appear to be only slightly higher than in the general population.

The most important mental health consequence appears to be the high rates of suicide attempts among people with kleptomania. In a large study of individuals with kleptomania, approximately one-fourth (24.3 percent) had attempted suicide. In 92.3 percent of those who attempted suicide, the attempts were attributed specifically to kleptomania. These findings underscore the importance of carefully assessing and monitoring suicidality in anyone who has kleptomania.

How common is kleptomania?

Many people have heard about kleptomania but have never known anyone personally with the problem. Is this because the behavior is uncommon? No national epidemiological study of kleptomania has been performed, but studies of kleptomania in various clinics around the world suggest that the disorder is fairly common. Studies of depressed patients found that 3.7 percent suffered from kleptomania; 3.8 percent of alcoholics also reported symptoms consistent with kleptomania; 2.1 to 5 percent of gamblers and 24 percent of bulimia patients had kleptomania. The behavior is not uncommon, and people with kleptomania should be helped to understand that they are not the only ones with this problem. Family members may also feel that no other family has ever dealt with this issue, so these numbers provide some perspective on the extent of the problem for them, too.

Anyone may develop kleptomania, and both men and women with kleptomania show substantial symptom severity and functional impairment. Most studies have found that women are more likely than men to have kleptomania. Compared with men, women with kleptomania are more likely to be married, to have a later age at shoplifting onset (21 versus 14 years of age), to steal household items, to hoard stolen items, and to have an eating disorder. Kleptomania is also a problem in all races and ethnicities, but whether and how it differs among races and ethnicities is not yet known. Studies from around the world suggest a common presentation regardless of culture.

Why don't more health care providers diagnose kleptomania?

Even though kleptomania is fairly common, health care providers fail to ask patients about any stealing behaviors they may have, and therefore the disorder often remains undiagnosed. If patients or their family members feel that the patient has a problem with shoplifting, they need to mention this to the clinician. Many factors explain why this severely distressing behavior is not diagnosed.

Shame and secrecy

Shame and secrecy are fundamental to kleptomania. Embarrassment and shame appear to explain, in part, why so few patients will volunteer information regarding these behaviors unless they are specifically asked. Often related to the shame and secrecy is the patient's misunderstanding of what a mental health care provider is required by law to report. Patients suffering from kleptomania may believe that the clinician is required to report their illegal behaviors. Health care providers have no duty to call police or stores. The information will be protected under doctor-patient confidentiality laws.

Patient lack of knowledge

Another possible reason for the failure to diagnose kleptomania is that patients often do not know that their behavior is a recognizable disorder that can be treated. Therefore patients may not volunteer the information, feeling that it is a "bad habit" or "character flaw" rather than a mental health issue.

Physician lack of knowledge

Few health care professionals, including mental health professionals, have education or training in kleptomania. If they do not know what to offer as help for it, health care providers will probably not ask about it. In addition, health care providers may have biases about stealing. For example, clinicians may see themselves as potential victims of the illegal behavior associated with kleptomania—that is, the health care provider pays more for items because of other people's shoplifting—and may not believe that the behavior is an illness and deserving of treatment.

Misdiagnosis

Kleptomania has many clinical similarities to other disorders, and this overlap in symptoms between kleptomania and other mental health problems may make diagnosis difficult. When combined with lack of knowledge regarding the clinical characteristics of kleptomania, the chance for misdiagnosis is considerable. Some of the more common misdiagnoses are discussed here.

Family members can be crucial in helping the clinician to make the correct diagnosis. They can often provide information about the history of other mental health problems, what they have observed more recently with the person, and whether the person is struggling with additional issues that she does not want to divulge (for example, drug addiction).

Mood disorder

Bipolar manic episodes are characterized by impulsive behaviors. A manic episode is when people are out of control, feeling too euphoric (or extremely irritable), and doing multiple impulsive behaviors that are getting them into trouble. These manic behaviors may include shoplifting, as seen in kleptomania. During a manic episode, however, people often exhibit multiple symptoms of mood dysregulation—excess energy, distractibility, elevation, or irritability—whereas the behavior of kleptomania usually is more specific and restricted in nature. To complicate the clinical picture further, individuals with kleptomania may also suffer from bipolar disorder. In such cases, it is important for the physician or therapist to determine if the shoplifting exists only during mania or simply worsens during a manic episode.

Other mood disorders may also be confused with kleptomania. Many people may report shoplifting only when they are feeling depressed. This may be a form of "self-medication" among some depressed individuals. This type of stealing would not merit the diagnosis of kleptomania. To complicate the diagnostic picture again, however, rates of depression are elevated in individuals with kleptomania, and there may in fact be subtypes of kleptomania among people who find mood elevation from their behavior and therefore "self-medicate" by stealing.

To summarize, there are depressed people who steal, and kleptomaniacs who are depressed. The clinical assessment should start with a history of how these two elements interact and have developed over time. In people whose behavior is affected by mood, the underlying mood difficulties should be treated, but the kleptomania may need additional treatment as well. Although the behavior may have been started to self-medicate the mood, the behavior may be maintained by a different mechanism.

Obsessive-compulsive disorder

There is often significant clinical overlap between obsessive-compulsive disorder and kleptomania. Patients may even refer to themselves as "obsessed" or engaged in shoplifting "compulsively." Although patients with kleptomania, like those with obsessive-compulsive disorder, may engage in their habits repetitively and be preoccupied with thoughts relating to their habits, the key difference is that people with kleptomania feel pleasure from the behavior, whereas obsessive-compulsive behaviors are generally done to alleviate anxiety. In OCD, symptoms tend to relate to cleanliness, contamination, symmetry, hoarding, or checking, unlike in kleptomania, where intrusive thoughts and compulsive acts relate specifically to stealing.

Substance addictions

Substance addictions frequently co-occur in people with kleptomania (between 20 and 45 percent of individuals). Health care providers need to determine whether (1) the substance abuse results in the shoplifting, perhaps through disinhibition (for example, shoplifting only when intoxicated); (2) the shoplifting, and the shame and desire to escape, causes the substance abuse (for example, shame over shoplifting leads to frequent drinking); or (3) they are two related but independent problems. It is sometimes too easy for health care providers to believe that all behaviors associated with drug or alcohol problems are minor or secondary events. But stealing may be primary and may be driving the person to use drugs or alcohol.

Personality disorders

Shoplifting may be one component in an otherwise complicated personality. The clinician has to try to find out whether the stealing merits an independent diagnosis of kleptomania or is secondary to a personality disorder. This can be particularly difficult in some cases, because borderline personality and antisocial personality disorders are characterized by impulsivity and violation of boundaries, as is kleptomania. Of course, it is not always a question of either/or, because kleptomania may co-occur with personality disorders. Clear separation of the behaviors may not be possible at first. The physician or therapist may need to make ongoing assessments over time to determine to what extent these various disorders interact in a patient.

Why does someone develop kleptomania?

Developmental issues

The past two centuries of kleptomania's history are littered with various theories and hypotheses that attempt to explain this baffling disorder, but researchers and physicians have not reached consensus on what causes it. Kleptomania has been interpreted as a reflection of unconscious defenses against anxiety, forbidden instincts or wishes, unresolved conflicts, prohibited sexual drives, fear of castration, and sexual arousal, gratification, and orgasm during the act of thievery, just to name a few. Although these causes possibly account for the stealing on an individual level for some people, no objective data support these theories.

Kleptomania's relationship with anxiety and depression has also been explored. The act of stealing has been interpreted as a risk-taking behavior performed by a depressed person that results in an elevated mood or that provides relief from stressful conditions. In children who report feeling injured or neglected, kleptomania may gratify two needs: the actions may be gratifying, and the stolen objects might dispel feelings of deprivation. There are no data, however, to confirm or refute any of these theories.

Family members, particularly parents, often attempt to explain why their child has this problem. Unfortunately, they also tend to beat themselves up about it, claiming they must have been bad parents or "done something wrong." We simply do not know the cause of kleptomania, and family members are often unsatisfied by the lack of explanation. We do know that some people with kleptomania have come from supportive loving homes and that others have been raised in more chaotic households. No parenting style or dysfunction has been consistently associated with kleptomania.

The kleptomania brain

As we discussed in chapter 1, there are multiple ways of examining the brain. One can study brain scans to see how the brain is formed and how it functions, and one can examine the chemicals in the brain to see if they are present at appropriate levels and are working properly. Multiple neurotransmitters, as well as familial and inherited factors, appear to play roles in the development of behavioral addictions.

We have limited knowledge about the brain in regard to kleptomania. We find it important for patients to have information about what we *do* know, however, as it gives them an understanding that their brain may be different from the brains of people who do not shoplift. This brain difference does not excuse the behavior, but it may allow the person to take the behavior more seriously and commit to treatment. Family members may also benefit from knowing some of this information, as it may dispel ideas that their loved ones are shoplifting because they are "bad."

Two areas of the brain that serve crucial functions in any motivated behavior are the ventral striatum (including the nucleus accumbens), which produces a drive to do something, and the frontal lobe, which allows us to consider the repercussions of our behavior and inhibit ourselves. Within these parts of the brain, multiple neurotransmitters help to coordinate information processing—these include serotonin, dopamine, and our natural opioid system. Low serotonin levels in the brain appear to correlate with high levels of impulsivity and sensation seeking, and there is some evidence that serotonin may be somewhat dysfunctional in kleptomania.

Dopamine is involved in rewarding and reinforcing behaviors. Reports from people treated with dopamine drugs for Parkinson's disease have also mentioned that some people started shoplifting. This provides clues about the role of this chemical in kleptomania.

Finally, urges linked to experiencing reward and pleasure are an important clinical target in kleptomania. Patients with kleptomania report urges to steal. Many indicate that the act of stealing reduces the urges or the tension these urges produce. Although many report the urges as intrusive, the act of stealing is a thrill for some, producing a pleasurable feeling. The opioid system in our brains is believed to control our urges through reward and pleasure processing. Naltrexone, a medication that blocks the opioid system in the brain, has shown benefit in treating kleptomania (see below) and thereby suggests that this system also is involved in the illness.

Neurocognitive testing of women with kleptomania has demonstrated that, as a group, they show no significant deficits in frontal lobe functioning (the brain region involved in making decisions, thinking about consequences, controlling behavior, and so on). Those individuals with greater kleptomania symptom severity, however, had significantly below average scores on at least one measure of executive functioning. Also, high rates of impulsivity were found in people with kleptomania. Cognitive problems in kleptomania may thus be more common with increasing severity of the illness.

Cases have been reported whereby someone developed kleptomania after the orbitofrontal circuits of the brain had been damaged. Brain imaging techniques have demonstrated decreased white matter integrity (that is, less efficient connections in the frontal areas of the brain) in individuals with kleptomania compared to controls. These images are consistent with findings of increased impulsivity and support the idea that at least some individuals with kleptomania may not be able to control their impulse to steal.

Psychological issues

Kleptomania is most likely caused by multiple variables (biological, psychological, sociocultural). Why do kleptomania patients continue to engage in a behavior that results in unneeded items when the possible repercussions are so devastating?

Focusing on the pleasure many patients derive from shoplifting, some have theorized that kleptomania results from an attempt to relieve feelings of depression through stimulation. Risk-taking behavior may therefore produce an antidepressant effect for some patients. It is possible that depressed individuals may engage in shoplifting to distract themselves from life stressors and unpleasant thoughts. Unlike drugs or alcohol, shoplifting leads neither to intoxication nor to a directly impaired ability to function at work, and as such, it may be an especially attractive means of escape.

Persons who are depressed may also view the objects they steal as a means of significant symptom relief and the possibility of being apprehended as a relatively minor and theoretical setback. Ironically, problems resulting directly from shoplifting (for example, embarrassment and shame from getting caught) may in turn lead to even more shoplifting as a misguided attempt to manage those feelings.

Because most people with depression do not shoplift, theories have been offered as to why some depressed people might engage in kleptomanic behavior. One theory has suggested that shoplifting is a symbolic attempt to make up for early deprivations or losses. The shoplifting may therefore be a symbolic compensation for an actual or perceived loss. Some support for this theory may be found in a recent study of parental bonding, which found that patients with kleptomania report that their parents were less likely to express affection than the parents of healthy controls. Furthermore, a recent family study found that patients with kleptomania were more likely than healthy controls to have a first-degree relative with alcoholism. We have evidence that the children of alcoholics experience increased psychological stress, so examining feelings of deprivation or loss in patients with kleptomania may be a productive way of looking at the problem.

Shoplifting provides a particularly rewarding experience: acquiring items without paying for them. The positive reinforcer in kleptomania is the acquisition of items for nothing. The fact that a person is not always able to shoplift due to store security and other factors makes kleptomanic behavior particularly likely to be reinforced and to persist over time. Physiological arousal associated with the shoplifting (that is, racing heart, sweating) may be yet another reinforcer that initiates and perpetuates the behavior.

Similarly, negative reinforcement (which involves removing a punishing stimulus) hypothesizes that initiating but not completing a habitual behavior leads to uncomfortable states of arousal. Applied to kleptomania, this would imply that shoplifting is performed to experience relief from the aversive arousal of urges. Even the self-medication theory of kleptomania may represent a negative reinforcement. This could account for why kleptomanic behavior continues even when the person is frequently apprehended.

In addition to a behavioral model, there may also be specific thinking errors directly linked to kleptomanic behavior: (1) believing that only shoplifting will reduce the urge or the depressive state; (2) selective memory (for example, remembering the thrill of shoplifting while ignoring the shame and embarrassment of being apprehended); and (3) errors in self-assessment (for example, people believing they deserve to get caught stealing because they are not intrinsically worth anything).

These psychological theories of kleptomania should be understood, however, in the context of the possible biological explanations for kleptomania. For example, although many people shoplift at some time in their lives, it remains to be explained why not all individuals who shoplift more than a few times succumb to the positive reinforcement of acquiring items or the negative reinforcement of relief from aversive arousal of urges. One simple possibility is that individual differences in brain biology might regulate the propensity to respond to the positive or negative reinforcement of shoplifting. That is, positive or negative reinforcement may have a more powerful influence on some individuals than others in terms of future kleptomanic behavior.

How is kleptomania treated?

It is unknown how many individuals suffering from kleptomania seek formal treatment. Treatment data for kleptomania are sparse. No medications have been approved by regulatory boards for the treatment of kleptomania, but pharmacotherapy has shown some early promise in treating this disorder.

At this time, the available treatments for kleptomania offered by mental health professionals include various forms of psychotherapy and pharmacotherapy, but studies exploring the efficacy of these treatments are extremely limited. Typically a patient will either do therapy only or will take medications in conjunction with therapy.

Psychotherapy

As discussed above, psychoanalytic and psychodynamic theories were initially used to try to understand kleptomania, and thus psychoanalytic and psychodynamic psychotherapy were the treatment of choice for many decades. How effective this treatment modality has been, however, is unknown, because there have not been any controlled studies. Some patients respond well to this type of therapy, sometimes in conjunction with medications, while others have shown no improvement despite years of therapy.

Cognitive behavioral therapy (CBT) may be a potentially promising treatment for kleptomania. Cognitive treatment focuses on modifying the maladaptive and distorted thoughts associated with stealing (for example, the belief that acquiring something will address internal distress). Behavioral therapy focuses on modifying behavior in response to triggers and distorted thinking patterns. In particular, several CBT strategies have been used to treat people with kleptomania: covert sensitization (for example, the patient is instructed to imagine herself stealing and then to imagine a negative outcome, such as being caught or feeling nauseated or short of breath), aversion therapy (for example, the patient is asked to engage in aversive breath holding until it becomes mildly painful whenever an urge to steal or an image of stealing is experienced), and systematic desensitization (helping the patient achieve a relaxed state through progressive muscle relaxation and asking the patient to imagine the different steps of the stealing episode, meanwhile suggesting that he could better control the urge to steal by controlling the anxiety).

We recently published on the successful use of six weekly sessions of CBT using imaginal desensitization (creating an audio recording of a client's "typical" stealing episode) plus motivational interviewing. Imaginal desensitization uses the idea of imagining the steps of stealing while maintaining a relaxed state or by including a negative mood induction element. The patient then imagines the potential scene of stealing but also imagines her ability not to steal in that context. The client in our case was instructed to listen to the recording several times a day between sessions and whenever an urge to steal presented itself. After successfully curbing his urges and stealing behaviors, the client completed maintenance sessions of therapy and reported no stealing at a six-month post-therapy follow-up. This particular therapy has been shown to be helpful for other behavioral addictions.

Finally, people have been successfully treated by learning to substitute alternative sources of satisfaction and excitement when they experience the urge to steal. Finding alternative sources of excitement, pleasure, and self-fulfillment is important if someone is going to avoid stealing in the longer term.

Medications

Medication can be combined successfully with therapy. Since people with kleptomania usually report uncontrollable urges to steal and excitement or a "rush" when stealing an item, an opioid antagonist, such as naltrex-one, may dampen the excitement and urges of kleptomania. Naltrexone is approved in the United States for the treatment of alcoholism and opioid addiction. At doses between 50 mg and 150 mg per day, naltrexone has shown benefit in reducing stealing urges and behavior. This dosing is usually higher than the FDA-approved dosing of 50 mg per day. The higher doses may result in liver toxicity, so anyone using the drug at higher doses needs to undergo regular blood work to make sure the liver is healthy. Individuals ideally should also avoid certain other medications known to increase the risk of liver toxicity. Naltrexone has been used by some people for several years without problems. When a person receives therapy for kleptomania, we recommend medication for a period of six to twelve months.

Although there is no clear indication for the use of antidepressants in kleptomania, the fact that depression and kleptomania often go hand in hand, and the fact that suicide attempts are common in individuals with kleptomania, suggests a potentially important role for antidepressants in treating this disorder.

Finally, two other medications may be beneficial for treating klepto-mania. Memantine, a medication used for treating dementia, has been investigated as a treatment for kleptomania with some promising results. Dosing has ranged from 10 to 20 mg per day. Individuals reported fewer urges to steal and less stealing behavior, and they demonstrated less impulsivity on cognitive tests. The anticonvulsant topiramate (100 to 150 mg/day) has also produced positive symptom relief in kleptomania. Topiramate has been used in research studies with some success for alcoholism, and so its use in kleptomania is based on stealing being an addictive behavior like alcoholism.

How long does a person have to take medication?

If someone has found a medication helpful, we recommend that the person stay on the medication for at least six months to one year. If the person's symptoms worsen after stopping the medication, it can be restarted and taken for another year.

Special issues in treatment

Several common situations may influence which treatment approach is best for a particular individual who has kleptomania.

1. If there is active substance use, the question is whether the person can be treated as an outpatient and the same approach used to treat the substance addiction and the kleptomania. If the substance use interferes with kleptomania treatment, the individual may need to be referred for detoxification or residential placement for the drug addiction before receiving the kleptomania-focused therapy.

2. Even if there are ongoing legal issues, the family and the patient need to be completely honest with the health care provider. If patients know they have a court appearance coming up, they often disclose only certain facts, but withholding facts does not make for optimal care. We usually tell patients we are treating that if they go to court or commit crimes during the treatment process, they should ask someone else do their court-ordered evaluation. Although the clinic notes could be given to their lawyer with the individual's permission, we recommend that the main clinician responsible for treating the kleptomania not testify on a patient's behalf.

3. Given the high rates of suicide and suicide attempts among individuals with kleptomania, the physician or therapist needs to assess for thoughts of suicide at each visit. When people become suicidal and are a threat to themselves, the treatment for kleptomania may need to be interrupted and the focus put on safety and suicide prevention. Inpatient hospitalization may be necessary.

Case

Greg is a 54-year-old married man with a full-time job. He had never seen anyone for a mental health problem before and denied having struggled with any mental health problems in the past. Greg did, however, report shoplifting for most of his life. The behavior started when he was about 12 years old and over the years had evolved into a weekly behavior. Greg tended to steal high-priced goods. After each theft, he left the item or items at the door of the store or donated them to charity. "I just like the theft. I don't want the things I steal." He reported having a stable marriage, a good job, and plenty of friends. He was baffled by his behavior, but he had thoughts or urges to steal very frequently, and the urges were temporarily eliminated by the actual thefts.

Greg was seeking help for this problem at this point in his life because he had almost been arrested by security recently. A security guard had stopped him after he took an expensive watch from the store. He explained that he "forgot" to pay for it, and the store accepted payment for the watch in lieu of arrest, likely because he was well dressed and a frequent shopper at that particular store.

Greg was initially nervous about discussing the stealing and mentioned only some vague "personal problems" for the first two visits. Later he said, "I was not sure I could trust you. I didn't want you calling the police on me." After again asking about professional limits on privacy with respect to what was reportable, he eventually told us his entire history. He was treated with naltrexone, 50 mg each day, and weekly CBT. Although he experienced a couple of lapses over the next four months, he dramatically reduced his behavior, reported significantly decreased urges to steal, and after six months was abstinent and has remained theft-free for the past three years.

Key Points for Individuals with Kleptomania

1. Kleptomania is a real mental health problem with promising treatment options.
2. You need to be honest with your health care provider about your behavior and the effects of the behavior.
3. Stay out of stores unless absolutely necessary. When you have to go to a store, go with a list and set a time limit and an alarm so that you do not stay in the store longer than absolutely necessary. Otherwise

shopping can be done online, or you could ask someone else to do the shopping for you.

4. Disclose your behavior to at least one family member or friend to have someone who can help you in the recovery process. Part of therapy is avoiding stores or going to stores with someone who can help monitor your behavior.

5. Go through everything in your house that is stolen and donate the items to charity or throw them out.

Key Points for Family Members

1. Family members should help the person stay out of stores by doing the shopping or by supervising the shopping.

2. Family members should ask to see the receipt of anything new brought into the home.

3. The person may do well at first in therapy, but as with Greg in the case above, this behavior has often gone on for years, and setbacks are common. The family should be encouraging and promote treatment in such cases but not excuse or condone the behavior.

5

Sex

Robert, a 38-year-old married man with two children, felt that he'd had a problem with pornography ever since he was an adolescent. He had started pornography use at about age 15 years and never stopped since. Over the last ten years, his use had increased, particularly with access to online pornography. He loved his wife and felt that they had a good sexual life with each other, but at night he would go online and look at pornography for hours. Recently, he became tired at work, and his boss asked why he was falling behind with his sales targets. This was the reason he came for treatment.

At age 20 years, Robert struggled to some extent with binge drinking while at college and had a couple of citations for driving under the influence of alcohol. He had curtailed his drinking since and had no other mental health issues. He was generally a happy person, had friends, and enjoyed his job. He could not understand how or why the pornography use had become so intense. He had no sexual abuse history, and even his taste in pornography was what he described as "fairly vanilla," meaning no kinky or paraphilic interests. Robert had wanted to come for treatment two years ago but was not even sure this was something that clinicians treated. After seeing a story about it on the news, he contacted our clinic.

Why should we be concerned about compulsive sexual behavior?

Pornography, which is just one part of compulsive sexual behavior, is a huge business, and as such, it is here to stay. Some estimates claim that the pornography business (online, video, and magazines) makes $10 billion to $14 billion in annual sales globally and that it is a bigger industry than all the major league sports and possibly even bigger than the Hollywood movie industry. Companies earn revenue by making adult movies available in people's homes and hotel rooms. There are many debates about the social and personal aspects of pornography, but what we know is that most people who use it can control their behavior. As with many of the behaviors discussed in this book, however, a portion of people cannot control their use of pornography. These individuals might have a problem referred to as compulsive sexual behavior.

Compulsive sexual behavior (CSB) is a term that characterizes repetitive and intense preoccupations with sexual fantasies, urges, and behaviors that are distressing to the individual and/or result in psychosocial impairment. Individuals with CSB often perceive their sexual behavior to be excessive but are unable to control it. They act out impulsively (act on impulses and lack impulse control) or compulsively (are plagued by intrusive obsessive thoughts and driven behaviors). CSB can involve fantasies and urges in addition to or in place of the behavior, but it must rise to a level of clinically significant distress and interference in one's daily life to qualify as a disorder.

Over the centuries, compulsive sexual behavior has gone by many names, such as hypersexuality, hyperphilia, erotomania, satyriasis, promiscuity, Don Juanism, Don Juanitaism, and more recently sexual addiction, impulsive-compulsive sexual behavior, and paraphilia-related disorder. The terminology has often implied different values, attitudes, and theoretical orientations.

Compulsive sexual behavior can generally be divided into two categories: paraphilic and nonparaphilic. Paraphilias (for example, fetishism, exhibitionism, sexual sadism, and pedophilia) are typically behaviors that have been deemed socially unacceptable. They may involve nonhuman objects, the suffering of one's self or a partner, or sex with children or a nonconsenting person. Nonparaphilic CSB, which is characterized by more typical sexual desires, includes compulsive sexual acts with multiple partners, constant fixation on a partner who may be considered unobtainable, compulsive masturbation, compulsive use of pornography, and compulsive sex and sexual acts within a consensual relationship. In this chapter, when we refer to compulsive sexual behavior, we are referring only to nonparaphilic behaviors.

Unlike some of the other behaviors in this book, nonparaphilic CSB is not currently recognized by the American Psychiatric Association in the *Diagnostic and Statistical Manual of Mental Disorders*, fifth edition (*DSM-5*). Although CSB was considered for inclusion, its inclusion was not approved. In fact, there was considerable debate about the disorder, whether it was a "real" problem, and what, if anything, it was similar to. Although *DSM-5* did not ultimately acknowledge CSB as an independent disorder, the World Health Organization (WHO) has recommended it be included in the forthcoming eleventh edition of the *International Classification of Diseases* as an impulse control disorder.

The WHO believes that diagnoses, such as CSB, that affect public health should be recognized. CSB is associated with sexually transmitted infections, including HIV infection, unintended pregnancies, viewing of pornography at home and in the workplace, and extensive cybersex users who use the Internet to seek partners. Thus, the WHO believes that it is clinically useful to view CSB as being related to other disorders that are also characterized by repeated failures to resist impulses, drives, or urges despite long-term harm.

Is compulsive sexual behavior a new disorder?

Because of the continually changing characterizations and terminologies for problematic sexual behavior, it is difficult to compare historical notions of CSB to what we currently think of as the behavior. Some forms of compulsive sexual behavior appear to date back centuries. The first medical accounts that we have found date to 1775, and the concept was later refined in 1845, when the term *nymphomania* was coined.

How is compulsive sexual behavior diagnosed?

Multiple behaviors are encompassed by the term *compulsive sexual behavior*. There are at least seven common behaviors: compulsive cruising for multiple partners, compulsive fixation on an unattainable partner, compulsive autoeroticism (masturbation), compulsive use of erotica, compulsive use of the Internet for sexual purposes, compulsive multiple love relationships, and compulsive sexuality in a relationship.

Most people who struggle with CSB are reluctant to mention it to their health care providers, and most physicians are generally uncomfortable talking about sex with their patients, in part because of a lack of training. People are more likely to bring up the topic when they are being treated for a sexually transmitted infection, an unwanted pregnancy, or marital or relationship problems. Other patients might seek treatment for anxiety, depression, or alcohol or drug abuse. There is a high rate of comorbidity between CSB and mental health problems, particularly anxiety disorders, depression, and substance abuse disorders. Therefore, when patients present with these types of problems, their health care providers must consider that sexual behavior might be associated as a coping mechanism, distressing outcome, or comorbid condition.

The essential feature of CSB is persistent and recurrent maladaptive sexual behavior that results in problems with work, school, or family life. To receive the diagnosis of CSB, an individual must have recurrent and intense sexual fantasies, sexual urges, and sexual behavior that result in some impairment in functioning as well as at least four of the following five symptoms during the same six-month period:

1. Spending excessive time consumed by sexual fantasies and urges as well as planning for and engaging in sexual behavior
2. Repetitively engaging in these sexual fantasies, urges, and behavior as a response to anxiety, depression, boredom, or irritability
3. Habitually engaging in sexual fantasies, urges, and behavior in response to stressful life events
4. Repeatedly but unsuccessfully attempting to control or significantly reduce these sexual fantasies, urges, and behavior

5. Continually engaging in sexual behavior without regard for the risk of physical or emotional harm to self or others

Important clinical aspects of CSB

The majority of people with CSB who seek treatment are males whose compulsive sexual behaviors began during late adolescence. Individuals with CSB typically experience a preoccupation with sexual fantasies or have uncontrollable distress-producing sexual urges that lead them to engage in repetitive, uncontrollable distress-producing sexual behavior.

Individuals with CSB cite certain mood states as triggers for the sexual behavior, most commonly sadness or depression, happiness, or loneliness. Furthermore, a majority of individuals with CSB may experience a dissociative state (feeling outside of one's body or detached from the world) while participating in compulsive sexual behaviors. After engaging in the behavior, most feel shame and experience a negative mood change, lasting anywhere from minutes to days. Even though the individuals dislike behaving and thinking in such a manner, CSB distracts them from other concerns, reduces anxiety or tension, improves mood, and makes them feel important, powerful, and excited in the short term.

Research has shown that individuals with CSB have an average of three different compulsive sexual behaviors. The most commonly reported compulsive sexual behaviors are masturbation, compulsive use of pornography, and protracted promiscuity or compulsive cruising and multiple relationships.

The Internet is another avenue for compulsive sexual behavior, because the Internet is available 24 hours a day, 7 days a week; is affordable; and is perceived to be anonymous. About 72 million people visit pornography websites annually, and research has shown that between 10 and 20 percent of those who use the Internet for sexual purposes have online sexual problems. Studies have shown that sexual compulsivity is strongly related to the amount of time spent pursuing online sexual activities. Online sexual activities include pornographic audio, video, and text stories; real-time chatting with fantasy partners; searching for a sex partner;

replying to sex advertisements; purchasing sex products; and contacting prostitutes.

Consequences of compulsive sexual behavior

Individuals with CSB may face a variety of medical complications, including unwanted pregnancies; sexually transmitted infections, including HIV/AIDS; and physical injuries due to repetitive sexual activities (for example, anal and vaginal trauma).

Sexually transmitted infections, such as HIV/AIDS, are a major health risk for those with CSB. Higher levels of sexual compulsivity appear to be related to more unprotected sexual acts, a higher total number of sexual partners, and being diagnosed with multiple sexually transmitted infections. A study of HIV-positive individuals found that compared with those who were not sexually compulsive, people with CSB were significantly more likely to report engaging in unprotected vaginal or anal intercourse, having more total sexual partners, and engaging in sexual behaviors that could lead to HIV transmission. In addition, four times as many new HIV infections can be expected in the HIV-negative partners of sexually compulsive individuals.

Individuals with CSB report significant marital, occupational, and financial difficulties as consequences of their sexual urges and behaviors. They also report that significant distress is caused by the amount of time spent consumed by their urges, thoughts, behaviors, out-of-control feelings, and post-behavior guilt. Mental health consequences, such as anxiety and depression, are common in people with CSB.

Although studies have documented the connection between substance use and sexual behaviors, few have specifically examined the connection between CSB and substance use. Substances can alter the experience of sexual behaviors. Methamphetamine increases sexual desire and sensations while decreasing sexual inhibition, and cocaine leads to feelings of well-being, self-confidence, and alertness. Research has shown that substance abuse is common in individuals with CSB, but it is not always clear which problem came first. Did the person become addicted to drugs because she was initially looking for sex and drugs came along with the sexual activity, or did the sexual activity get out of control because of the drug addiction?

The substance abuse–sex connection may be stronger among gay men due to the higher rates of certain drugs of abuse in the gay community (e.g., crystal methamphetamine) and the arguably easier access to sexual outlets. In addition, substance users typically feel more confident and desirable, and they have an easier time cruising for sex and making contact with another person, resulting in greater success in finding a partner. One study examining drug use in African American men who have sex with other men found that drug use increased their feelings of hypersexuality or sexual compulsion, increased their comfort with approaching other men, and allowed them to cope with feelings of homophobia.

Is compulsive sexual behavior the same as being a "pervert" or a danger to children?

CSB is not the same as a paraphilia (a category of sexual behavior that is often linked to the term "pervert," which has a derogatory connotation and should not be used). CSB involves normative sexual behavior, whereas the paraphilias involve sexual behaviors that are not only impulsive or compulsive and repetitive, but also unconventional or socially unacceptable.

Paraphilias may involve illegal behavior, such as an adult having sex with a minor. Not all sexual offenses, however, are committed by people meeting diagnostic criteria for a paraphilia. That said, many paraphilias interfere with a person's psychological or interpersonal functioning. The eight paraphilic disorders listed in the DSM-5 are pedophilia (interest in children), exhibitionism (exposing oneself), voyeurism (watching others in sexual situations), sexual sadism (humiliating others), sexual masochism (being humiliated), fetishism (finding an object sexual), transvestic fetishism (cross-dressing), and frotteurism (rubbing against people).

One important note about pedophilia, and any sexual behavior that involves underage individuals, is that physicians and psychologists are mandated by law to report suspected maltreatment or abuse of children and adolescents.

How much sex is too much sex?

Normal sexual behavior may be overpathologized (that is, treated as disordered when it is not) if a clinician fails to recognize the wide range of normal human sexual expression—not only in frequency but also in variety. Overpathologizing can also occur among family members and health care providers who possess overly conservative attitudes and values regarding sexual expression. It is important for people who feel they have CSB to find a professional they are comfortable with when it comes to discussing a wide range of sexual behavior. They should consider seeking consultation from a specialist in sexuality. Patients who see a clinician who is not well educated about sexuality may end up feeling more embarrassment and shame than they did before the appointment.

Some individuals, with their own restrictive values, will diagnose themselves with this disorder, thus creating their own distress. Therefore, it is very important to distinguish between people who have a values conflict with their sexual behavior and those who engage in sexual behaviors that are driven by impulsive, obsessive, or compulsive mechanisms. For example, one man who came to our clinic did so because he masturbated once every few weeks but felt that any masturbation was "sinful and perverted." In this case, "treatment" consisted of simply explaining to him the range of sexual behaviors that are normal and healthy, including his own.

There is an inherent danger in diagnosing CSB simply because someone's behavior does not fit the values of the individual, group, or society. There has been a long tradition of pathologizing behavior that is not normative within a culture. For example, masturbation, oral sex, homosexual behavior, viewing pornography, or having an extra-relational affair could be viewed as compulsive behaviors because someone might disapprove of these behaviors. There is no scientific merit, however, to viewing these behaviors as disordered, compulsive, or "deviant." When people are distressed about these behaviors, they are most likely experiencing a conflict with their own or someone else's value system rather than suffering compulsive sexual behavior.

Behaviors that are in conflict with someone's value system may be problematic but not necessarily out of the person's control. Sexual problems are often caused by a number of nonpathological factors. People may make mistakes. They may lack awareness of the law. They may, at times, act impulsively. Their behavior may cause problems in a relationship. Some people use sex as a coping mechanism similar to the use of alcohol, drugs, or eating. This pattern of sexual behavior may become problematic. Problematic sexual behavior is often remedied, however, by time, experience, education, or brief counseling.

Not all excessive sexual behavior is compulsive sexual behavior

Just because someone is hypersexual does not mean he or she has CSB. Other problems may result in a person becoming hypersexual. The first thing to keep in mind is that not all excessive sexual behavior equals CSB. As we mentioned above, sexual behaviors that are in conflict with someone's own value system or someone else's value system may feel problematic, but they are not compulsive. Similarly, just because someone has more sex than someone else does not mean that CSB is involved. The value system of the patient and the family may get confused with CSB. CSB must also be distinguished from the excessive sexual behavior that is often seen in new relationships. In those situations, the excessive sexual behavior is usually time limited and does not typically cause distress or result in impairment.

Extreme cases of sexual behavior (for example, masturbating six times a day and being unable to get to work on time due to the masturbation) are the easy cases to diagnose. It is more difficult to assess and diagnose behaviors that fall into the gray area. Take the example of a young man who is not working and spends hours each day looking at pornography. Is his behavior due to CSB or simply to excess free time? This is where the list of diagnostic criteria earlier in this chapter can be very useful. It is also a simple question of how much control the young man has over his behavior. If a job comes up, and he can stop his behavior and function at a high level, then he probably does not have CSB.

Excessive sexual behavior can occur as part of a manic episode in a person who has bipolar disorder. A manic episode is when a person is out of control, feeling too euphoric (or extremely irritable), and doing multiple impulsive behaviors that are getting her into trouble. Sexual behavior may be one of those impulsive behaviors. If the problematic sexual behavior also occurs when the person's mood is stable, the individual may have CSB in addition to bipolar disorder. This distinction is important because the treatment for bipolar disorder is very different from that for CSB.

Excessive sexual behavior can occur when a person is high on drugs. In particular, stimulants (such as cocaine, amphetamines) as well as gamma hydroxyl butyrate (GHB) have resulted in excessive sexual behavior. If the sexual behavior does not occur when the person is not taking drugs, then the appropriate diagnosis would likely not be CSB.

Finally, it is important to find out whether the person started being hypersexual after beginning any medications. Some patients taking certain medications (for example, medications for Parkinson's disease or restless leg syndrome, or aripiprazole to treat depression or psychosis) may engage in hypersexual behavior. These medications may increase dopamine in a specific part of the brain that controls our urges and our need for rewarding stimulation. If the sexual behavior decreases or stops when the medication is reduced in dosage or stopped, then a diagnosis of CSB would not be indicated.

How common is compulsive sexual behavior?

Evaluating the prevalence of CSB is difficult because of the embarrassment and shame frequently reported by those with CSB as well as society's (at times) judgmental position toward the expression of sexuality. Although no large epidemiological studies have been performed, the estimated prevalence rate of CSB is approximately 3 to 6 percent. One recent study of public university students found that 2 percent (3 percent of men, 1.2 percent of women) met the diagnostic criteria for CSB.

Can anyone develop CSB?

Gender

Both men and women can develop this problem, although most studies have found that the majority of individuals with CSB who seek treatment are male. Most people with CSB develop the illness during late adolescence. Because of the sensitive nature of sexual behavior, however, the prevalence of CSB may be underreported in the general population, and females may be underrepresented in these clinical samples. A recent study found that 3.1 percent of women who responded to an online survey were characterized as hypersexual. Another found that 5 percent of women reported having some problems with Internet sexual behavior. These studies highlight the importance of bearing in mind that CSB can occur in both genders.

Several factors may influence the gender disparity in CSB. First, the majority of individuals seeking treatment for CSB are males, and compared to men, women experience more CSB-related shame. Many women with CSB may not seek treatment, or shame may keep women from acting on their sexual impulses. Second, research has found that compared with females, males have more sexual fantasies, masturbate more frequently, become aroused more easily, and have more casual attitudes toward sex. Males also more often engage in sexual relations for pleasure and esteem reasons, whereas females participate in sexual relations to further their relationships and to develop long-term commitments for child-rearing purposes. Another factor that may contribute to the higher proportion of CSB in males is the cultural double standard that men who are highly sexual are labeled as being "men," while women who behave in a similar fashion are viewed as promiscuous.

Given that males and females may pursue sexual relations for differing reasons, it is possible that CSB presents differently in females. For many women, being in a relationship may be more enticing than the sexual activity. Women may therefore be more likely to engage in multiple love relationships rather than in compulsive "cruising" or having multiple superficially connected partners.

Age

A national study of risky behaviors among youth in grades nine through twelve in private and public U.S. schools (youths aged 14 to 18 years) indicated that 47.8 percent of students had participated in sexual intercourse, 7.1 percent of students had participated in sexual intercourse before the age of 13 years, 14.9 percent of students had participated in sexual intercourse with four or more individuals in their life, and 35 percent of students had participated in sexual intercourse with at least one person during the three months prior to the survey. With the increased rates of sexual activity in this age range, will we see more CSB as well? Little research has explored the area of adolescent CSB. One study found that 4.9 percent of adolescents in a psychiatric inpatient unit had a comorbid diagnosis of CSB. To date, this is the only known empirical study assessing rates of CSB within an adolescent population, and it was limited to psychiatric patients.

Ethnicity and culture

There is virtually no research devoted to ethnic and cultural aspects of CSB. One study found elevated rates of CSB types of behavior among a Hasidic Jewish inpatient population compared with non-Hasidic Jewish subjects. This research suggests that even in communities with ostensibly very rigid views of sexuality, behaviors consistent with CSB can be present. There is no evidence, in general, that individuals from particular cultures are significantly more or less likely to develop CSB.

GLBT community

In studies measuring sexual compulsivity, between 20 and 28 percent of GLBT (gay, lesbian, bisexual, transgender) individuals scored high on sexual compulsivity measures. In addition, men who have sex with men (who may in fact not identify as GLBT) appear to have significantly higher sexual compulsivity scores than women who have sex with women. Some researchers have suggested that sexual compulsivity may be more frequent in the gay and bisexual male community because of the availability of gay-oriented sexual outlets, such as sex parties, bathhouses, and sex websites.

Sexual compulsivity has been associated with sexually risky behaviors in both homosexuals and heterosexuals. One study comparing gay men to inner-city low-income heterosexual men and women found that sexual compulsivity was significantly associated with unprotected intercourse, total number of sexual partners, and sexual sensation seeking in both gay men and heterosexual individuals. Compared to heterosexual males and females, however, gay men were more likely to report inconsistent condom use and multiple sex partners.

Another study of 180 inner-city men with HIV who self-identified as gay or bisexual found that compared to those with low sexual compulsivity, men with high levels of sexual compulsivity were more likely to have unprotected intercourse and less likely to disclose their HIV status.

When asked about reasons for their sexual compulsivity, gay and bisexual men give both intrinsic reasons (such as poor mental health, low self-esteem, need for validation and affection, stress reduction, and biological predisposition) and extrinsic reasons (such as relationship issues, availability of sex, childhood sexual abuse, and maladjusted parental relationships). Other studies of CSB within the GLBT community have linked higher levels of internalized homophobia with greater sexual compulsivity.

Why does someone develop compulsive sexual behavior?

The role of the family

Substance abuse is common in the relatives of individuals with CSB. In a survey of people with CSB, most participants had experienced at least one substance addiction in their family. In fact, only 13 percent of individuals with CSB come from a family without a substance addiction. How should we interpret these data? One interpretation is that CSB may have a familial or even a genetic link to substance addictions. Another interpretation, which is not mutually exclusive to the first, is that certain family environments due to (or associated with) addictions may contribute to someone developing CSB.

Research suggests that most people with CSB come from families that have stressful dynamics. Restrictive environments regarding sexuality and dysfunctional attitudes about sex and intimacy may contribute to the later development of CSB. One theory concerning CSB and family interactions suggests that as children, the needs of those who would later develop CSB were not met because of either parental rigidity or lack of follow-through, resulting in the children believing that people are unreliable and that they can only depend on themselves. Sex therefore becomes a source of well-being to these individuals.

Several studies have also linked the development of CSB to childhood abuse. Emotional, sexual, and physical abuse histories have been reported in large percentages of individuals with CSB. Rates of childhood abuse in people with CSB may be three to four times higher than in people without CSB. Although causality between adult CSB and childhood experiences has not been established, an assessment of CSB may also warrant further investigation into an individual's familial relations and developmental background.

Biological variables

The onset of CSB has been linked to various conditions, including head traumas, brain surgeries, mental health illnesses, both prescription and nonprescription medications, frontal lobe lesions, temporal lobe epilepsy, dementia, multiple sclerosis, and the treatment of Parkinson's disease with dopamine drugs. That said, most cases of CSB do not have such a known biological cause.

Several studies have examined serum testosterone and sexual activity in CSB. In adult males, testosterone is secreted in *pulsatile* fashion (i.e., pulsating, throbbing), with the pulse height and frequency varying slightly throughout the day and at different times of the year. Research, however, suggests that frequency of sexual activity and level of sexual interest in those with CSB do not correlate with serum testosterone concentrations.

In terms of neurocognitive functioning, research findings have been inconsistent. One study found maladaptive cognitive processes and perceptions about sex in a population of homosexual and bisexual men compared with heterosexual men. A different study with heterosexual, homosexual, and bisexual men found additional potential cognitive differences, where mindfulness (being present "in the moment" during a negative experience) was inversely related to hypersexuality, which generated higher levels of impulsiveness and negative emotions. Finally, a small study examining impulsivity in young adults with CSB found no cognitive differences when compared to healthy control subjects.

Brain scans of people with CSB have produced interesting findings, but it is unclear how, if at all, we can use the information to help people with CSB. When presented with cues of varying sexual content, individuals with CSB reported greater sexual desire and had increased brain activity in areas associated with desire and emotions, the same regions shown in studies to be affected by triggers to drug cravings.

How is compulsive sexual behavior treated?

The first step in treatment begins with accurate diagnosis. To make an accurate diagnosis, the physician or therapist must first rule out medical causes of CSB (although rarely present, these causes are generally more likely when the onset of CSB has been abrupt or when CSB starts later in life in a person with no previous history of CSB). Certain neurological disorders can cause an individual to act inappropriately and possibly engage in CSB. Some of the most common examples are Alzheimer's disease (sexual disinhibition due to the effects of the disease on the frontal and temporal lobes, with a prevalence of between 4.3 and 9 percent of patients), Pick disease (impairs the regulation of socially acceptable behaviors), and Kleine-Levin syndrome (causes hypersomnia, which can lead to abnormal behavior such as hypersexuality). In addition, certain types of medications or illicit drugs can result in an increased sexual drive, such as dopamine agonists used to treat Parkinson's disease or cocaine, GHB, or methamphetamine.

When CSB is suspected, the patient and family members will do best if they find a specialist in the area of sexual behavior for assessment and treatment. Sources of referral are the American Association of Sexuality Educators, Counselors and Therapists (www.aasect.org) and the Society for Sex Therapy and Research (www.sstarnet.org).

Sometimes people simply need to understand the patterns of their behavior and its negative consequences to help motivate them to engage in healthier sexual behaviors. For people who feel that normative sexual behavior is somehow pathological, the physician or therapist can educate them about the normative range of sexual expression. Disagreements based on value system differences between couples are also common. These disagreements can be acknowledged, and the couple can work to find compromise solutions for handling their different values, just as is done with value conflicts in raising children, in family relations, or in managing finances.

It is also important to recognize that some people with CSB simply get better on their own. Known as *natural recovery*, this occurs in many addictions as well as in CSB. It is unclear in advance, however, who can ultimately control their behavior without any interventions. Some data suggest that people with mild cases of the disorder and those early on in the course of illness have better potential for natural recovery. One thought is that these individuals are performing a type of cognitive behavioral therapy on themselves. The idea of correcting cognitive distortions and replacing problematic sexual behaviors with healthy behaviors is not unknown to people even without therapy. Although natural recovery may occur, on the individual level, the possibility for it needs to be balanced by the current levels of distress and dysfunction of the person.

Psychotherapy

Many people need psychotherapy to treat compulsive sexual behavior. CSB is often deeply rooted and stems from a failure of healthy psychosexual development. Many people with CSB have grown up in challenging family environments and have underlying identity and intimacy problems. Many have lacked nurturance, love, acceptance, and positive role models. As a result, their psychosexual development has been adversely affected, which has ultimately prevented them from feeling good about themselves as sexual beings and led to problems with intimacy.

One of us (JEG) was trained in the treatment of CSB by Dr. Eli Colman's group at the University of Minnesota's Program on Human Sexuality. Although controlled studies in psychotherapy for CSB are lacking, expert physicians and therapists have been treating individuals with CSB for many years. Based on these years of experience, the preferred modality in that facility was group therapy combined with adjunctive individual and family therapy. Weekly group therapy is useful to examine how a person learns from others' coping strategies and develops new intimacy skills. Group therapy reduces the intense feelings of shame, too. Using an ongoing group, new members are able to learn from others who have almost completed and are able to understand the whole course of therapy. The group also provides peer support for improved coping.

Individual therapy, often involving a mix of cognitive behavioral therapy, supportive therapy, and even an analysis of family and interpersonal dynamics, allow the patient to address personal issues in greater depth. Individual therapy also allows for addressing issues that come up in group sessions. Family therapy focuses on family of origin issues and conflicts in interpersonal functioning. Family therapy can also focus on rebuilding trust within relationships, which is often damaged by a person's sexual behavior.

Goals of treatment

A goal of therapy is to work toward gaining some control over the problematic sexual behavior. To start, it is most practical to focus on controlling the person's most problematic sexual behaviors, for example, those that increase the risk for serious health problems, such as HIV. This process takes time. Given the general impulsive nature of many people with CSB, the idea of taking time to have gradual control over one's behavior may be unsatisfying and may be the reason for dropping out of treatment.

Therefore, the patient and the therapist should set realistic goals at the beginning of therapy.

One other issue is that, because of the shame caused by the behavior, many patients will set unrealistically rigid goals for themselves. For example, they may decide, "No masturbation ever." Some of this rigid goal setting is driven by overly restrictive attitudes about sexual expression—the same attitudes that may have been one of the driving forces responsible for the person developing CSB. Another factor in setting rigid goals is the need to feel good about oneself. When the goal is too rigid and unrealistic, however, it can backfire. People need to learn how to accept their sexual feelings and to feel good about themselves, regardless of their sexual behavior.

Because the goal of sexual behavior therapy cannot realistically be abstinence, the person needs to be able to define sexual boundaries of acceptable and unacceptable behavior. This is an important process taking place between the therapist and the patient. The patient must be involved in setting these boundaries, and a consensus should be established between therapist and patient. The role of the therapist is to challenge overly restrictive and overly liberal boundaries. The next step is to set goals for staying within those agreed-on boundaries, such as deciding which sexual behaviors are within the boundaries and which are outside them.

Many people are distressed when they try not to engage in their sexual behaviors. Some feel like they cannot cope with distress or that they grieve the loss of their best friend (much like an alcoholic may refer to the bottle as his best friend). Their distress may lead them to feel anxious or depressed. Coping with these feelings in therapy is essential, because unless they are effectively addressed, these emotions can lead to relapse.

Because CSB often reflects an underlying disturbance in identity and intimacy, another goal of therapy is to help people to develop a healthier understanding of themselves overall as intimate beings. Developing a healthier understanding of oneself may require addressing body image issues, which often come up in treatment. Many individuals with CSB are deeply insecure about their appearance and whether they are attractive. CSB creates a fleeting good sense of oneself: "If they have sex with me, then I must be attractive." The person's level of body obsession may be consistent with a body dysmorphic disorder or an eating disorder, but generally speaking, it is simply a profound lack of self-worth reflected by body image and attractiveness concerns. Cognitive therapy focusing on attractiveness helps many patients deal with these concerns.

To address problems with intimacy and to identify cognitive distortions that maintain CSB, patients are asked to write their sexual autobiographies, which include information about their histories of sexual activities, such as age of first sexual behavior, history of intimate relationships, and problematic or traumatic sexual experiences. The therapist and the patient then discuss patterns of behavior and address maladaptive patterns that the patient has developed. Recognizing these patterns allows people to understand how situations or emotional states may trigger their CSB. They can then recognize a sequence of events that lead to and perpetuate their CSB. By recognizing the cycle, a person can learn how to interrupt it. Relapse prevention strategies are used for this purpose.

Can medication help?

Though many people with CSB are resistant to the idea of medication, it can be extremely helpful in reducing CSB urges and behaviors. When people with CSB understand possible biological causes of CSB, as well as the side effects and possible benefits of medication, they may find the use of medication more appealing. There have been very few randomized clinical trials, however, and therefore physicians mostly depend on expert opinion in prescribing. None of the medications that we use now are FDA approved for CSB, which means that any medications we use are referred to as *off-label*. In addition, these medications might not be as helpful to patients with multiple other mental health problems that could be contributing to CSB. Medication may make psychotherapy more beneficial, however. Therapy often temporarily provokes anxiety or depression, and medications may help people cope with the emotional response to therapy.

Which medications might be helpful for overcoming compulsive sexual behavior?

The most frequently used medications are the selective serotonin reuptake inhibitors (SSRIs), a class of antidepressant medications. These medications have been shown to be effective in treating depression and anxiety and are often helpful for people with CSB. These medications also seem to help with impulse control, and their primary side effects are decreased libido—which can help in controlling CSB behaviors. When used for treating CSB, the SSRIs (often just at the recommended starting doses) may be useful in reducing the desire for sex, frequency of masturbation, and time spent using pornography. One potential caveat of SSRIs is that with some people, a decreased ability to have an orgasm may result in problematic sexual behaviors. For these people, the riskiness of the sexual behavior may be ramped up, to override the sexual side effects. For these people, the medication needs to be used in combination with therapy.

Naltrexone, an opioid antagonist, has also shown benefit in treating people with CSB. At between 50 mg and 100 mg per day, naltrexone has been effective in reducing urges in similar behavioral addictions and in reducing relapse in alcohol and opiate addiction. Not only does naltrexone seem to block the sensation- and pleasure-seeking aspects of the behavior, it may be helpful for treating general impulsivity as well.

Lithium and antiepileptics may also provide some benefit in CSB treatment. These medications have been used in the past and are still potentially effective treatments. In some patients for whom the SSRIs are insufficient in controlling their CSB, these medications can be used instead of or in addition to an SSRI.

Finally, in people with more resistant behaviors, antiandrogens can be used. These medications control libido and help with sexual urges, but they produce more severe side effects. They are a potentially useful medication option when other interventions do not work, but they should be considered a last resort approach and be used only in the most severe cases, when therapy has not helped, under specialist guidance.

What about support groups?

Sex Addicts Anonymous (SAA) is one support group whose purpose is to help people with sex addiction find recovery. This organization operates similarly to Alcoholics Anonymous (AA), with a focus on the twelve-step program. Another support group is Sex and Love Addicts Anonymous (SLAA), which is similar to both SAA and AA. There are no data on how well people do when attending SAA or SLAA, and so we advise individuals to seek individual or group therapy and then use these support groups for additional support and information.

Special issues in treatment

Several common situations may influence how we treat someone with CSB.

1. If there is active substance use, such as crystal methamphetamine, the question is whether the person can be treated as an outpatient using the same approach to treat the substance addiction and CSB. If the substance use interferes with CSB treatment, the individual may need to be referred for detoxification or residential placement for the drug addiction before receiving the CSB-focused therapy.
2. When an individual with CSB also exhibits clear signs of mania, this symptom needs to be addressed. The mania will need to be treated before the person can take full advantage of the treatment for CSB; indeed, the CSB may resolve when the manic episode is over or has been successfully treated. In most cases, treating the mania will involve medication to stabilize mood.
3. When individuals with CSB have significant personality disorders, such as narcissistic personality disorder, the standard treatment plan for CSB may need to be modified to include more psychodynamic approaches.

Case

Donald is a 24-year-old gay man who has been sexually active for almost ten years. He has multiple partners each day because it helps him feel good about himself. "I feel attractive and wanted when someone has sex with me." His behavior has put him in dangerous situations, such as the time he was robbed and raped. He is also currently concerned that he may have contracted HIV from a recent sexual act.

Donald started group therapy for CSB. Initially uncomfortable being gay in a group with many heterosexual men, he gradually grew to enjoy the support. In addition, he began taking naltrexone (50 mg per day) to reduce his sexual urges so that he could take part in the group discussions more effectively. "The medication helped me to be able to focus on what other people were saying in group, whereas before, I found myself constantly thinking about sex." In individual therapy, Donald has focused on body image issues and intimacy problems.

Over the course of his year-long treatment, Donald continued to do well. He was able to set boundaries of acceptable and unacceptable sexual behaviors and stick with those boundaries. He had a negative HIV test. The fear of getting HIV has continued to be a motivating factor in his care.

Key Points for Individuals with Compulsive Sexual Behavior

1. Compulsive sexual behavior is a real mental health problem with promising treatment options.
2. Recognize that issues such as low self-esteem and body image problems often make it more likely that a person will develop the disorder.
3. Prioritize both physical safety and sexual safety. Getting frequent testing for HIV and other STIs is important.
4. Stay off websites that promote easy sexual hookups; stay away from drugs and alcohol if they contribute to making impulsive sexual decisions; and find new healthy behaviors to take the place of sexual behaviors.

Key Points for Family Members

1. Family members need to provide a nonjudgmental atmosphere where the person can discuss sexual behavior and sexual health.
2. Family members should consider blocking websites that the person routinely uses for sex and provide opportunities for the person to reconnect socially with healthy loved ones and friends.

6

Internet

anny is a 19-year-old university student in the top 10 percent of his class who works part time as a laboratory assistant. He has many close friends and a good relationship with his family. He lives in a dormitory, where he shares a living room with five other friends but has his own bedroom. The pressures of a full school load combined with working ten hours every week have "ramped up" his stress levels, Danny says. His friends often go out drinking in the evening, but Danny avoids drinking alcohol because his father is an alcoholic. Alone in the dorm, Danny spends his evenings on the Internet watching videos, in chat rooms, and on online auction sites.

Over the past few months, Danny has become enraptured with viral videos. "I had a really stressful couple of days a few months ago. I came back to my room, and my friend had posted a funny video that made me laugh and really relieved my stress. I felt so good that I looked for more videos, and before I knew it, I had spent seven hours online. Now I go online first thing in the morning and am in a hurry to get back to my room after class to see what else I can find." Danny reports that he has started to miss classes, and his grades are suffering. He has become more and more isolated from his friends, who do not share his affinity for viral videos. He was fired from his part-time job for not being focused on the work. Danny reports that while he is upset about losing his job, he is happy to have more time to cruise the Internet. "I wish I had the extra money, but it works out just fine. I will just spend more time in my room, which will save me money." Danny has lost contact with a number of his good friends, and his academic career continues to spiral downward. The dean's office wrote to Danny's mother, informing her of Danny's poor performance. She takes Danny to the doctor for help, though he is reluctant to go.

Why should we care about Internet addiction?

The Internet is a relatively new feature in industrialized society, with use and access exploding over the past twenty years. The use, and potential misuse, of the Internet, has only gained attention in the very recent past, although the first reports of "computer addiction" were described in the 1980s. With more people having nearly constant access to the web through computers, tablets, and smartphones, individuals who appear unable to control their time on the Internet are starting to attract the attention of family, friends, and clinicians.

People who are addicted to the Internet have more physical and mental health problems, are more depressed, have more educational or occupational difficulties, and experience far higher rates of family and social problems than typical users. It appears that adolescents are disproportionately affected by Internet addiction. Several countries, including China and South Korea, consider Internet addiction to be an epidemic and a significant threat to teenagers. Even the American Medical Association wrote that Internet addiction posed a growing threat to individuals in American culture. Considering that the adolescent brain is still maturing and continues to mature through the age of 25, better understanding of the cause and effects of Internet addiction should be a public health priority in an ever-expanding, electronically connected world.

What is the difference between spending a lot of time on the Internet and addiction?

- "Isn't spending too much time on the Internet simply loneliness or depression?"
- "Sure, my teenager spends a lot of time on the Internet, but isn't that normal for teens these days?"
- "My wife spends a lot of time on the Internet, but it's nearly always on shopping sites. Does she have a problem with the Internet or does she have a shopping problem?"

The answer to each of these questions reflects the complicated nature of trying to figure out where "normal" Internet use ends and addiction begins. There is no set amount of time spent on the Internet that is considered *too* much. It really varies by the individual. A few factors should be considered when a person or family member is trying to determine if the person has a problem with the Internet. The first is context: *why* is the person online? For people who make their career in social media marketing, for example, their livelihood is based on being online. They may spend a minimum of eight or more hours online each day. Second, what level of distress or dysfunction does the time spent online cause the individual? As our case example demonstrates, Danny's use of the Internet caused significant problems with his grades, he lost his job and friends, and he became increasingly isolated.

Is Internet addiction a real mental health problem?

Internet addiction (also called problematic Internet use) has not been formally included as a mental health problem in the fifth edition of the *Diagnostic and Statistical Manual of Mental Disorders*. Although Internet addiction is absent from the *DSM-5*, a new disorder called "Internet Gaming Disorder (IGD)" is included as a "condition for further study." As indicated by the name, IGD is characterized by compulsive use of the Internet to play games, use that leads to impairment and is reported as distressing to the individual. The criteria for IGD can be summarized as meeting at least five of the following within the past year:

1. A preoccupation with playing Internet games (*not* gambling, which is classified under gambling disorder) in which the Internet gaming becomes the focal activity of the individual's life
2. Irritability, sadness, or other "withdrawal" symptoms when the person is restricted or prohibited from engaging in Internet gaming
3. Increasing amount of time gaming (known as *tolerance*)
4. Unsuccessful attempts to cut back on or quit Internet gaming
5. Loss of interest or participation in previously enjoyed activities because of Internet gaming
6. Continued engagement in Internet gaming despite consequences
7. Deceiving others about the amount of time spent Internet gaming
8. Internet gaming to escape a bad mood, guilt, anxiety, and so on
9. Risking loss of a significant opportunity (job, educational, etc.) because of Internet gaming

Proposed criteria for Internet addiction are extremely similar to those for IGD. The main components of problematic Internet use are behavior that is uncontrollable, causes distress, is time consuming, results in untoward or negative consequences, and is not due to another mental health problem.

How common is Internet addiction?

Prevalence studies for Internet addiction have mainly focused on adolescents and have primarily been conducted in Asian and European countries. The consensus, however, is that Internet addiction is a worldwide problem. Samples of a broad age range of individuals have indicated a prevalence of Internet addiction ranging from 0.3 percent to 6 percent of the population. Internet addiction may occur in about 4.4 percent of all adolescents and young adults.

Clinical aspects of Internet addiction

Whether Internet addiction is more common in men than women is still a matter of debate and is dependent on several factors, including culture and local (or other) accessibility to the Internet. The large European study of nearly 12,000 adolescents in eleven countries noted that Internet addiction was far more common in boys (5.2 percent versus 3.8 percent of girls). The same study found, however, that maladaptive use of the Internet (meaning problematic but not meeting full proposed criteria for Internet addiction) was more common in females (14.3 percent) than males (12.4 percent). Culture plays a role, as it often does: surveys of adolescents in Hong Kong found higher rates of Internet addiction among females, and a Swiss study found no gender differences.

It has been proposed that males in general may be more likely to have Internet addiction because of their higher likelihood of engaging in online gaming, cybersex, and gambling.

With the Internet becoming more accessible to younger people, one concerning prospect is that problematic Internet use may begin at increasingly earlier ages. As reported earlier, China considers Internet addiction to be one of the top threats to its teenage population. Reports of children sleeping with their smartphones rather than teddy bears have permeated the news in many countries throughout the world. In South Korea, a country leading the way with over 98 percent of households connected to the Internet, an estimated 160,000 children (ages 5 to 9 years) are addicted to smartphones, tablets, or computers.

Why does someone develop Internet addiction?

As with many mental health disorders, the explanation for why someone develops Internet addiction is largely conjecture at this time. Other addiction research tells us that a combination of genetic (that is, family history of addiction) and environmental (stress, access to the addictive substance or behavior, and so on) factors are involved in the development of addiction. People with a family history of addiction, for example, are more genetically vulnerable and require less of an environmental influence to develop an addiction. Conversely, those without such a history require a higher level of environmental factors to push them toward an addictive behavior.

Think of walking across a gorge on a bridge. Those with a family history have a much narrower bridge to walk across, and small influences from around the bridge make it more likely that they will fall off. Those without a family history have a much wider, more stable bridge, but strong influences from around the bridge may still knock the individual off the bridge and into an addictive state.

There have been no longitudinal studies following people from before they develop addiction until they develop an addiction. Instead, studies have looked at associations between people who have an Internet addiction and their environmental risks. The large European study of nearly 12,000 adolescents, for example, noted that those with Internet addiction were more likely not to live with a biological parent or relative, to be an only child, not to have a steady boyfriend or girlfriend, and to have a perceived low rate of parental involvement in their lives. These results do not answer the question of *why* someone develops a problem with the Internet. Future long-term population-based studies with genetic research may help us understand why some individuals but not others develop Internet addiction when exposed to the Internet.

The biology of Internet addiction

Brain imaging, using techniques like magnetic resonance imaging (MRI), can help us better understand the brain of a person with an Internet problem. Unlike many other behavioral addictions, Internet addiction has been the subject of a substantial amount of neuroimaging research in recent years, especially in Asian countries. Most research has focused on Internet gaming addiction, and findings are that those with Internet addiction have brains that are different. Certain areas of their brains activate when they are presented with Internet-related stimuli, while this is not true for those without Internet addiction.

Based on the research to date, it appears that Internet addiction is biologically similar to other behavioral and substance addictions. In particular, certain areas of the brain (for example, the prefrontal area involved in appropriate social functioning, judgment, and problem solving, as well as the cortico-striatal areas involved in regulating planned, flexible, goal-oriented behaviors) are quite different in those with an Internet addiction than in those without. These areas of the brain are important in processing and inhibiting behaviors because they are the decision-making centers of the brain. In fact, several studies have found that people with Internet addiction have poor decision-making processing when compared with individuals who are able to use the Internet in a nonpathological way. The question remains as to whether differences in the brain exist *before* the onset of an Internet addiction and drive the behavior, or whether Internet addiction causes the brain to change over time.

How do I know it is Internet addiction and not a different problem?

A number of other mental health problems may involve the compulsive use of the Internet. Understanding what factors are driving the use may provide clues to what the real problem is.

For example, people with significant anxiety about their health report spending countless hours researching perceived health problems in an effort to better understand or validate their symptoms. Treatment for such an individual would likely involve restricting or prohibiting Internet use (in the short term) and not reinforcing the belief that they are ill (or will become ill).

Attention deficit hyperactivity disorder (ADHD) is also common in people with Internet addiction, although they are not the same disorder. Studies have found that children and adolescents with ADHD are more likely to have an Internet addiction. The Internet provides those with ADHD a source of constant stimulation, instant reward, and the ability to maintain a state of hyperfocus over a long period. The Internet may even function as a means of self-treatment in some ways. Online gaming, for example, has been shown to stimulate the release of dopamine in the brain—dopamine is deficient in those with ADHD, and the dopamine deficiency may be "treated" by online gaming. People with ADHD also have problems with self-control (often called "inhibition deficits"), which may make it harder for them to limit their Internet use or tear themselves away from the computer once they have started. To differentiate ADHD from Internet addiction, the person or family members need to ask whether the individual has problems focusing on other tasks or not paying attention when spoken to; whether the person avoids tasks that require sustained mental effort; and whether the individual is easily distracted or forgetful in daily activities. These are just a few of the questions that can help to identify ADHD. For ADHD, there are likely to be symptoms of inattention, hyperactivity, and/or impulsivity dating back to childhood, rather than problems just restricted to use of the Internet.

Similarly, with the rise in online shopping over the past ten years, many patients report spending a very large amount of time (sometimes more than twelve hours daily) shopping online. They not only shop and spend but also scour the Internet for deals, such as coupons, a better price, or the "perfect" gift. Anyone spending this much time in these activities should be screened for compulsive buying disorder. Some individuals report significant distress and difficulties from both the time and the money spent shopping online. An individual with an Internet shopping problem may have both an Internet addiction *and* a compulsive buying problem (see chapter 8). What is important, however, is determining which behavior promotes the other.

The same logic holds true for an online gambler who reports significant consequences from the time and money spent gambling online, or for someone who is on the Internet for sex. Individuals who spend a disproportionate amount of time on the Internet yet spend most of that time looking at pornography or gambling may have larger problems with these behaviors than with the Internet itself. In these cases, the Internet is simply a means of getting at the addiction and is not the addiction itself.

Consequences of Internet addiction

While some might believe that Internet addiction is a harmless disorder, it has truly significant and negative consequences in the daily lives of those affected. Minor physical problems include dry eyes or blurred vision, but this addiction can also lead to sleep deprivation from continued use, poor nutrition, and fatigue at school or at work. These consequences can lead to lost productivity, job loss, academic difficulties, and marital problems caused by irritability and arguments over time spent online. As Danny reported, "I would often come home from class, eager to spend time online. Before I knew it, it was four in the morning. I would try to go to sleep but kept thinking about how my Internet session didn't feel complete, so I would get up again. I would skip class the next day to catch up on sleep and then do it all over again." An extremely long online gaming session was even noted as contributing to the death of a 28-year-old male.

Mental health

As with many mental health problems, people with Internet addiction may have multiple problems that tend to occur with each other. Whether one problem precedes another problem, however, is often hard to determine. This poses the "chicken or the egg" conundrum for many mental health problems, including Internet addiction and other disorders that often co-occur in people who have depression, anxiety disorders, substance abuse or dependence, or ADHD. For example, with Internet addiction and depression, the central question is whether the development of an addiction to the Internet resulted in the person becoming depressed, or whether a depression (which is often associated with self-isolation and sleep problems) resulted in the person spending more time on the Internet, in their isolation and poor mood. Sometimes it is unclear. This is where family members can be extremely helpful, often giving clear descriptions of what they have noticed.

Family, social life, and academics

Many individuals who consult us because they have problematic Internet use have significant consequences from their Internet use, including arguments in the family, social isolation, and school problems. Danny, who was a high academic achiever and had a good relationship with both family and friends, is typical of a young individual with Internet addiction. Like many people with addictions, Danny had poor insight into his problem: "I might not spend as much time with my friends as I used to, but they respect my interests. And my failing grades are not due to my Internet use but because my classes are extremely hard and the tests are unfair." Many people justify their use of the Internet by pointing out perceived positive reasons for using the Internet, while ignoring the negatives. For example, as Danny says, "The Internet helps me learn things that my books do not explain well. I talk to my family all the time with video calling as well. If anything, the Internet helps me more than hurts me." A close analysis of a person's Internet use, however, often reveals that use for classes and talking to friends is less than 10 percent of overall use. Such cognitive distortions are common in Internet addiction and may be why most people do not think they have a problem. It is often the job of family members to discuss what they have seen and bring forward their concerns for the person.

How is Internet addiction treated?

Despite a high prevalence of Internet addiction in Asian and some Western nations, our knowledge of effective nonmedication and medication treatments for Internet addiction is quite limited. Most people with Internet addiction do not seek treatment because of several factors, including shame or embarrassment and a belief that their compulsive Internet use is not problematic. Parents may believe that their child being on the Internet most of the time is "normal" for teens and thus do not intervene.

Therapy

One of the most common and effective therapies used for Internet addiction is cognitive behavioral therapy (CBT). As the name implies, CBT focuses both on individuals' cognitive processing (for example, how they think through problems, their thoughts about their behavior, what thoughts precede and follow a behavior) and on their behavior (for example, what they are doing, when and how often they engage in the behavior). In cognitive behavioral therapy, patients work through how they think about problems and what happens before, during, and after they engage in their problem behavior. They have homework exercises, in which they monitor and record their thoughts and actions between sessions. A recent analysis of all treatments for Internet addiction concluded that CBT was the treatment of choice. It also noted, however, that any psychotherapy is better than doing nothing. CBT has been effective for adolescents with Internet addiction.

Another treatment approach has used group therapy for both the person with Internet addiction and their family members. Therapy decreases the severity of the Internet addiction and builds better relationships with family members. In fact, family support appears to be a vital part of the treatment of Internet addiction, especially in adolescents, as it helps develop positive adolescent-parent communication and positive management strategies.

Medications

There is very limited evidence at this time for the treatment of Internet addiction with medications. Currently, no medications are approved by any regulatory committee worldwide for the treatment of Internet addiction. Studies using antidepressants have not shown success. When Internet addiction co-occurs with ADHD, stimulant medications seem to demonstrate benefit for both problems. Given the limited information available on the use of medications for Internet addiction, we cannot recommend a specific medication at this time.

Residential treatment

Although inpatient treatment centers (where the individual stays overnight and receives treatment throughout the day, usually for a month) are rare for Internet addiction, such places may be useful if the person is unwilling to do outpatient therapy or lacks motivation to work on the behavior on his own. These programs offer a safe environment where the individual is completely unplugged from the Internet. There is currently no evidence that residential treatment results in better outcomes than individual counseling, but individuals and their family should be aware that these facilities are available.

We are aware of two residential treatment centers: the Center for Internet Addiction (netaddiction.com) and reSTART (www.netaddiction recovery.com). More details about both are available in the resources section of this book.

Treatment recommendations

The first-line treatment for an individual with Internet addiction is CBT. If CBT is not available, however, other forms of psychotherapy may be useful. Treatment should aim to include family members whenever possible and to evaluate and treat co-occurring mental health conditions. There are no medications at this time that we would recommend as an initial treatment for Internet addiction itself; however, for those individuals reporting significant urges to engage in the Internet or a family history of addiction, "anti-craving" medications, such as the opiate antagonist naltrexone, should be considered.

Because Internet addiction is often associated with a number of other co-occurring problems, the individual with the Internet problem and the family should tell the health care provider about any other mental health problems that are currently an issue or were a problem in the past. Understanding how the Internet use relates to these other problems may be important to target the treatment appropriately.

Support groups

Support groups based on the twelve-step model of Alcoholics Anonymous (AA) are available and should be encouraged for those wanting to connect with others going through a similar experience with Internet addiction. Internet and Tech Addiction Anonymous (ITAA) (www.netaddiction anon.org) and On-Line Gamers Anonymous (OLGA) (www.olganon.org)

provide forums in which individuals or family members of those with an Internet addiction can share their experiences and provide support to each other. As with more established programs like AA, those interested in ITAA or OLGA should find a meeting that they feel comfortable attending. Although the principles of all meetings center on the twelve-step model, not all meetings are the same in terms of age, gender, or background. Some meetings may be specific to teens, women only, and so forth.

Goals of treatment

It is unreasonable and unrealistic to expect that patients either will or should abstain from all Internet use, just as those with compulsive buying behavior need to buy some things, those with food addiction must eat, and those with sexual addiction continue to engage in sexual activities. A reduced or *controlled* use of the Internet should be considered the long-term goal of treatment. In the acute phase of treatment, however, patients may need to abstain from their primary focus of Internet use and from the means by which they access the Internet. For example, if the central medium of addiction is a smartphone, the individual in treatment should be expected to abstain from all Internet use on the smartphone during the initial weeks of treatment. The patient may use a mobile phone without Internet capabilities. If a computer is the main medium of addiction, placing significant restrictions on time (as agreed on between therapist and patient) and placing restrictions on sites to be visited (for example, e-mail only) can help. Over time, the patient will likely be able to integrate more time and access into their Internet use; however, in the first stages of treatment, time and access should be restricted as much as possible.

What if treatment does not work?

Addictive behaviors such as Internet addiction are often difficult to treat, and treatment failure or inadequate response is common. If treatment fails, the potential causes of failure need to be addressed and the situation reassessed before a new course of treatment is begun. One factor in success is whether the person has adequate family or social support.

Another question is how motivated the person is to change the behavior. Just because the person is experiencing significant consequences for her Internet use does not necessarily indicate that she is ready to change her behavior. Sometimes family members are more concerned with the behavior than the person with the problem. Family members may need to wait until the person has even more significant consequences before she is ready to do something about the problem.

Prevention strategies

Countries like South Korea, where nearly all households have broadband Internet and more than 75 percent have smartphones, have led the way in early prevention strategies for children. Children as young as 3 years old are taught about the dangers associated with overusing the Internet, and more than 90 percent of children in kindergarten are taught to control their use of online devices. As with most activities children engage in, their exposure to the Internet should be monitored and limited.

Although connected devices such as tablets are increasingly being used as educational tools, or less prudently, as entertainment for children, the debate on how much is too much is only beginning. The debate parallels the one surrounding television, where the same question arises: how much television is *too* much television?

Properly monitoring and limiting exposure for children to set amounts of time and ensuring that caretakers also model proper behavior is vital in helping to prevent Internet addiction. If children see their mother or father constantly checking their phone, on the computer, or sleeping with their smartphone on the nightstand, the children will believe that this is normal and acceptable behavior. Why should they behave differently?

Parents should make sure that the Internet is used for educational purposes *at least* as much as it is used for recreational purposes. We would recommend a much higher amount of educational use than recreational use, but this decision is obviously based on the discretion of the parents.

None of this is to minimize the benefits of the Internet. It can be an extremely valuable tool that provides an endless source of education and knowledge for children. Ensuring that they learn proper Internet use and also engage in many activities that do not involve using the Internet, however, will help children to learn proper use and potentially decrease the risks of developing addictive use.

Case

Jennifer is a 16-year-old high school student with two older brothers. She is a good student and is involved in many school activities, including running and debate club. She received a smartphone for her birthday because her parents wanted her to have a phone when driving, in case she broke down and needed to call for help. Her friends all have smartphones, and they text message each other during the evening and while at school. Jennifer also started using the Internet more in her room at night, chatting with friends. Having an unlimited messaging plan, her parents never noticed a problem until Jennifer was involved in a car accident, and the investigating police officer suspected texting was involved at the time of the crash. The accident injured another driver. Jennifer's lawyer recommended that she see a psychologist as a matter of due diligence, to assess for problematic texting and Internet use.

The psychologist asked the parents to bring their detailed cell phone records since Jennifer's birthday to her first appointment. Her parents were shocked to note that she had texted her friends thousands of times over the preceding month, starting at 6:30 a.m. and lasting until 3:00 a.m. at times. A review of her computer use noted a similar pattern of compulsive use. When asked about her texting and Internet use, Jennifer told the therapist adamantly, "I do not have a problem. All of my friends are the same way, and we still get good grades. Yes, my grades might have dropped in the past few months, but that's just because I'm not good at my current courses. The accident was not my fault either. My friend texted me, and I was just being a good friend by responding."

Jennifer very reluctantly agreed to have her phone limited to calling capability only and to move her computer, which had been in her room, to a common area of the house. She had weekly therapy sessions, in which she learned coping skills and proper interaction with peers (such as the benefits and detriments of constant contact with friends). Her parents also agreed to limit their smartphone use, to promote a sense of family and teamwork. After six weeks of therapy, Jennifer reported that she felt ashamed of how her behavior had caused harm to others (the car accident) and that she realized most of her messaging and Internet use was nonessential and, in fact, prevented her from focusing on her schoolwork—schoolwork that she actually enjoyed. Feeling that Jennifer was mentally more in control of her phone and Internet use, her parents agreed to give her a smartphone back, but with limits on its use. Jennifer's grades have improved, and she says she feels much better about her life.

Key Points for Individuals with Internet Addiction

1. Do an honest assessment of how much time you spend each day on the Internet in nonessential ways, and how it is affecting your life.
2. Limit yourself to one modality of Internet use, such as a computer, and remove Internet capability from cell phones.
3. Block or disable certain Internet features that have occupied the most time.
4. Use the Internet only in common areas at home, not in the bedroom, and set strict time limits for use (perhaps using an alarm when the time is up).
5. Develop other activities in life. Exercise, read, and do other things to remember that there is more to each day than the Internet.

Key Points for Family Members

1. Family members should model using the Internet responsibly.
2. Family members should help set time limits on Internet use, remind the person of other activities, and even remove the computer or other devices from the person when they notice excessive use.
3. Family should encourage other sources of fun, information gathering, and socializing.

7

Food

Theresa is a university student who since her early teens has had episodes of eating that make her feel out of control. She gained a lot of weight in high school, and her self-esteem plummeted. Other students bullied her at school because of her weight, and she felt ashamed of her appearance, not helped by all the images she saw of "perfect women" on television and in magazines. In high school another student gave her laxatives, and Theresa used them to try to lose weight, but she no longer does this.

Theresa had not seen a doctor for many years, but a college friend encouraged her to make an appointment with her family physician. Theresa admitted to the doctor that she had been overconsuming food almost daily for the past six months. The eating episodes were getting more intense. During each episode, Theresa would consume large amounts of food in a short period, including chocolate and ice cream. She described the urge to do this as irresistible and said that the eating is pleasurable, but that immediately afterward, she regrets it. In addition, she felt frequent stomach pain due to bloating, and she had trouble breathing when walking up stairs. Since the overconsumption began, Theresa had gained more weight, and she now avoided social contact because of embarrassment. Her family doctor calculated her body mass index (weight in kilograms divided by the square of her height in meters) at 32, putting her weight in the obese range. Theresa had hidden the behavior from her parents and younger sister, whom she lives with, although they had noticed her weight gain.

After taking a detailed history, doing a physical examination, and ordering blood tests, Theresa's doctor referred her to a dietitian. Theresa also agreed to weekly sessions of cognitive behavioral therapy from a psychologist. Her doctor discussed medication options, but Theresa preferred to try therapy first. With therapy Theresa was able to gradually gain more control over her food consumption, and the out-of-control eating episodes occurred only about once a month. She successfully lost weight and was able to get her body mass index down to the normal range. Theresa gained confidence and started to socialize again.

Why is food addiction a concern?

Food addiction is important because of its potential consequences: it is associated with a great deal of psychological distress and multiple physical health problems. For example, food addiction is strongly associated with obesity, one of the leading causes of disability and mortality (premature death) worldwide. Unfortunately, the majority of people with food addiction have not sought help for their illnesses.

Food addiction, also called "eating addiction," refers to eating a larger amount of food than intended, continued eating despite knowing the adverse effects, and a persistent desire or an unsuccessful effort to control the excessive eating. Although we all occasionally eat large amounts of food at one time and may regret doing so, food addiction differs from problematic overeating because food addiction is associated with more significant eating, greater impulsivity, and less ability to act in accordance with personal goals. There is some overlap between food addiction and other disorders—obesity, binge-eating disorder, and bulimia nervosa.

Essentially, eating becomes addictive when it is repetitive, when the person feels compelled to do the act or finds it impossible to resist, and when there are functional consequences associated with the behavior. People with food addiction may or may not binge on food. Bingeing on food is a central symptom for binge-eating disorder, in which a person consumes large amounts of food in a relatively short period. People may meet the above criteria for food addiction but not the criteria for binge-eating disorder. That is, individuals may feel out of control in their consumption of large quantities of food, but they may do this in a more general way, rather than in discrete "bingeing" episodes. It is also important to bear in mind that a person can be obese but not meet criteria for "food addiction" and vice versa.

How common is food addiction?

The World Health Organization (WHO) estimates that by 2030, 57.8 percent of the world's population will be obese. Many people with obesity suffer from food addiction, which is common: approximately 5 to 8 percent of the world's population experiences some form of food addiction at some point in life. Eating disorders occur across socioeconomic, cultural, and geographical divides. They are not the preserve of the wealthy, women, or the westernized world. Atypical eating behaviors are a growing problem in young people, and though they are more common in women, the gender divide in terms of prevalence is much smaller than once was thought.

Is food addiction a recently recognized phenomenon?

Atypical eating behaviors have existed for centuries, although the rates of eating disorders likely have varied considerably across time, probably because of variations in the social and environmental factors that affect behavior. In the Middle Ages, people from wealthy families would gorge themselves with vast quantities of food and then vomit so they could consume more; this behavior did not necessarily constitute food addiction, because the behaviors were limited to certain situations, were culturally endorsed, and (one assumes) occurred without the subjective loss of control that would be characteristic of the modern understanding of the condition.

In 1956, the physician and allergist Theron G. Randolph first defined food addiction as a specific adaptation to one or more regularly consumed foods to which a person is highly sensitive, leading to excess food consumption and symptoms that are similar to those of other addictive processes. In this first description of food addiction, the addictive consumption of food involved corn, wheat, coffee, milk, eggs, and potatoes. Food addiction does not always equate with sweet cravings.

The term *food addiction* has since been used in combination with specific eating behaviors to describe an abnormal pattern of excessive consumption. Though behavioral addictions such as gambling have been recently recognized by the fifth edition of the *Diagnostic and Statistical Manual of Mental Disorders* (DSM-5), there is still no consensus that food addiction is a clinical disorder, nor is there a universally accepted definition for food addiction. With this shift in recognition and the medicalization of eating disorders, there has also been a change in how they are understood: traditionally, eating disorders were regarded as being a product of society, cultural pressures, or family dynamics, but now it is recognized that genetic and other biological influences are also important.

How is food addiction diagnosed?

Diagnosing a food addiction can be more challenging than diagnosing many other psychiatric conditions. There are no objective tests (such as blood markers, cognitive tests, or brain scans) that can make or refute a diagnosis, so the diagnosis relies on a physician or therapist doing a careful interview with the individual. Provided the person being assessed is comfortable with the situation, it can be helpful to obtain additional information from a loved one, such as a partner or close family member. Many patients do not agree to allow the clinician to talk with loved ones, however, because they may feel ashamed of their symptoms or be reluctant to share them with others. Some people with food addiction are incredibly adept at hiding their behaviors from others and minimizing them, which can make diagnosis and treatment very challenging, even for experienced experts in the field.

For the diagnosis of food addiction, we look for these behaviors:

1. Eating larger amounts of food than initially intended or over a longer period than intended
2. A persistent desire, or unsuccessful attempts, to cut down
3. Continued overconsumption despite knowledge of consequences
4. Giving up activities because of food use
5. A craving or a strong desire to eat specific types of foods

What are the outcomes for people with food addiction?

Food addiction commonly begins during adolescence, with peak age of onset being 14 to 20 years of age, but food addiction can begin at any age. The majority of affected individuals do not seek professional help until years after the symptoms begin, if they seek help at all. Community studies show that people with food addiction typically come into contact with various health care professionals in adulthood, but they are usually seeing the clinician for treatment of the consequences of food addiction rather than for treatment of the food addiction itself. For example, someone with food addiction may develop depression because of the effects of the condition, and then see the family doctor for treatment of depression, or develop obesity and see the doctor for treatment of obesity, without ever disclosing the underlying food addiction.

Health consequences of food addiction

Because our nutritional status influences all organ systems in the human body (including the brain), food addiction has potentially serious medical consequences, and comprehensive medical assessment is very important. For people who think they might have a food addiction, a vital first step is to tell a health care professional. Disclosing this information can seem daunting, especially when considering the list of medical problems that can arise from overconsumption. But it is better to get a checkup to know whether anything is wrong so that something can be done about it if so.

When doctors are concerned that patients may have a food addiction, they conduct a detailed screening and medical assessment, to avoid overlooking any health consequences of the weight gain that often come with food addiction. Physical examination, along with measurement of weight, height, and blood pressure, should be done. From the weight and height, the person's body mass index (BMI) is calculated. The BMI is calculated by dividing the weight in kilograms by the height in meters squared, or by dividing the weight in pounds by height in inches squared, then multiplying by a conversion factor of 703. (You can find BMI calculators on the Internet.) The BMI gives an indication of whether individuals are underweight or overweight for their given age and gender.

There are circumstances in which the BMI is not a good indication of nutritional status, especially in children and in muscular individuals, who may weigh more because of their muscle mass. The health care professional should also order a blood test to check cholesterol and blood sugar (to test for diabetes) as well as a heart trace (EKG/ECG).

Psychological consequences of overconsumption

Food addiction involves a loss of self-control, which leads to not only difficulties stopping the behavior, but also, for many, a sense of shame and guilt. As with most behavioral addictions, with food addiction it is common for family members or other loved ones to have trouble understanding the problem. They may tell the person to "snap out of it" or "just stop it." This reinforces the sense of shame and hopelessness associated with eating, which paradoxically makes it harder to control the symptoms. It is perhaps not surprising, then, that many people who have a food addiction also have mental health conditions such as depression and anxiety disorders. The longer the untreated food addiction lasts, the greater the risk the person has of developing other mental health issues. Although depression or anxiety might lead people to see their family doctor, they may not tell the doctor about the underlying food addiction.

A related psychological feature of food addiction is being impulsive. Increased impulsive or addictive traits, including symptoms of attention deficit hyperactivity disorder in childhood and post-traumatic stress disorder in women, have been associated with food addiction. Food addiction is also linked with emotional dysregulation, meaning a person has difficulty modulating his emotions.

Food addiction is associated with decreased quality of life, particularly with respect to health, self-esteem, interpersonal relationships, work, and social functioning. It is well established that addictive behaviors such as food addiction are associated with increased use of health services and higher numbers of days taken off from work. The extent of functional impairment appears to be more strongly related to the current severity of disease than to other factors such as gender, educational level, or how or when the disorder first began. Food addiction can also affect family life and finances if caregiving must be provided for the person with the food addiction. In health care systems requiring individuals to pay directly for their health care cost, many people with food addiction suffer economic hardship because of this expense.

Why is food addiction under-recognized and undertreated?

People with food addiction often do not get the help they need, or they get this help only when they have had the condition for a number of years. There are a few reasons for this.

Social extremes are normalized

We live in a social climate that places great pressure on people (especially adolescents) to appear a certain way. Images of celebrities are digitally altered to make them appear perfect. While our televisions, stores, and the Internet remind us of the need to be healthy and "live forever," unhealthy food is everywhere, and take-out foods are advertised constantly. People with food addiction often experience guilt for not achieving the "perfect" body image, but because many people in the westernized world are now obese, those with obesity may not perceive themselves to be different from their peers. Both guilt and normalization of obesity may deter someone from seeking treatment.

Lack of knowledge

Some people with food addiction do not know that their behavior may represent a recognizable disorder for which treatments are available. This is not the fault of the individual: education about food addiction is often lacking in educational settings and public health campaigns.

Clinician lack of knowledge

Relatively few health care professionals have education or training in food addiction. This lack of training, as well as the complexities of diagnosing and treating food addiction, can mean overlooking this condition or being unaware of how to treat it.

Shame and secrecy

Shame and secrecy are common in people with food addiction. Even members of the person's household are often unaware of the underlying behaviors and problems the person is experiencing. Someone who is ashamed and secretive is much less likely to seek health care for a food addiction.

Why does someone develop a food addiction?

There is not a single straightforward cause of food addiction. In the past, and even to some extent in the modern day, many people held the belief that problems with overconsumption were simply a product of the sociocultural context—that they stemmed from modern Western society's widespread promotion and availability of unhealthy foods. In actuality, food addiction is likely to be a product of a complex interaction of genetic, biological, and environmental factors.

Is it the person or the food?

Certain foods have rewarding and reinforcing properties, and these rewarding properties increase our motivation to seek these foods out. The more rewarding the food, the less able we are to restrain ourselves. Processed foods are designed to maximize palatability and reward, and to create exciting sensory experiences using taste, flavor, smell, and texture. The diets of people with food addiction usually contain a broad range of different foods, particularly many of the rewarding and reinforcing types of food (for example, foods with a perfect balance of fat and sweet). Some researchers have suggested that perhaps access to a diversity of foods, especially a diverse range of highly palatable foods, is the prerequisite to developing a food addiction.

Genetics

Genetic factors are influential in the development of substance addictions and may play a role in food addiction as well. Twin or family studies of food addiction, however, have not yet been performed.

Personality

Individuals with food addiction exhibit signs of being impulsive. This suggests that they may act without thinking, display difficulties stopping their behavior, and in general prefer immediate pleasures over delayed rewards. People with food addiction also tend to score high on measures of neuroticism, which have demonstrated a general vulnerability to all sorts of addictions. High scores on neuroticism reflect elevated levels of emotional reactivity, susceptibility to stress, and negative mood.

What might be happening in the food-addicted brain?

Consuming food is necessary to sustain life and involves brain regions that are ancient in evolutionary terms. The intestinal tract itself is almost like a "second brain," in that it contains vast amounts of neurons used to transmit and process sensory information; indeed, the intestinal tract contains more of the neurotransmitter serotonin than the brain does. Signals from the body, including from the intestinal tract but also from the bloodstream (for example, signals about glucose levels), are transmitted to the brain to help regulate appetite and hunger. Another key aspect of circuitry involved in eating is the brain reward system (including the nucleus accumbens), which is regulated by neurotransmitters such as dopamine, opioids, noradrenaline, and serotonin. One part of the brain (the prefrontal cortex) helps to regulate our behavior and to control our tendencies to crave certain foods, allowing us to flexibly adapt our behavior rather than getting stuck in repetitive habits. Food addiction most likely involves dysregulation of the brain's reward system, the brain's regulation center within the prefrontal cortex, and the intestinal tract. It would be incorrect to suggest that everyone with a food addiction has the same brain or body problems. As noted above, no specific scientific investigations, such as blood tests, cognitive tests, or brain scans, can reliably detect someone with food addiction.

How is food addiction treated?

Treatments fall into the categories of psychotherapy or medication, although ideally, people should have access to both.

Psychotherapy

For food addiction, the strongest evidence to date in terms of psychotherapy supports the use of cognitive behavioral therapy (CBT). CBT helps to reduce the intensity and duration of eating episodes as well as addressing cognitive distortions focused on food cravings, weight, and eating. Disappointingly, CBT does not usually lead to marked weight loss, and for this reason, it is critical to target obesity in food addiction with additional treatments originally developed just for obesity (such as medically supervised dietary restrictions, exercise, and behavioral weight-loss treatment). Self-help programs for food addiction may be useful as an extra route of support, but they are less well researched than CBT and should not be the first treatment tried.

Medications

When considering any medication for food addiction, the patient and clinician should discuss the benefits and risks. The physician would need to consider any pre-existing medical conditions, other medications the person is taking, any history of allergies, and the patient's preference. For children, psychotherapy treatment is preferable to medication. For adults, medication may be considered as augmenting therapy or, when preferred by the patient, instead of therapy.

There have been no formal studies of medication for food addiction, and therefore physicians tend to use the medications that have helped in other behavioral or substance addictions. Medications such as topiramate, naltrexone, or *N*-acetylcysteine may all help reduce urges to over-consume food items. Many people ask about stimulant medications because they reduce appetite and may help people lose weight. There are few data about their use in food addiction. If someone has found a medication helpful for food addiction, we recommend that the person stay on the medication for at least one year. If the person's symptoms worsen after stopping the medication, it can be restarted and taken for another year.

Case

Rufus is a 22-year-old store assistant who went to see his family physician after becoming depressed and feeling that he was not able to go to work. Initially he was reluctant to discuss factors that could be contributing to his depression. Thanks to the sensitive way in which the physician talked with him, Rufus eventually admitted that he was being bullied at work about being overweight. When asked about his dietary patterns, Rufus described feeling out of control with his eating: he was craving certain types of foods—anything high in sugar, such as cola and cake—and he spent a great deal of time searching for these products, which he ate in the middle of the night. When he stopped eating these foodstuffs, he kept thinking about them all the time, and he found the urge to eat very difficult to resist. Despite putting on weight and feeling faint from time to time, he had been unable to stop, and he had been eating more and more over time.

After a physical checkup, Rufus was found to have a borderline high glucose test, meaning that he was at risk of developing diabetes in the future. His blood pressure was also higher than expected for his age, meaning that he would be at higher than usual risk of heart and other health problems in the long term.

Rufus had support from his family physician and was referred to a psychologist, who began working with Rufus using cognitive behavioral therapy specifically tailored for food addiction and depressive thought processes. He also started a course of the antidepressant fluoxetine, a selective serotonin reuptake inhibitor (SSRI). He saw his family physician regularly for physical and mental health checkups. With time, his food addiction symptoms improved, he could control his calorie intake, and he was able to go back to work. In retrospect he wished he had gone for help sooner. Rufus was pleased to see that his blood pressure and glucose were back within the normal range during his latest checkup with his doctor.

Key Points for Individuals with Food Addiction

1. Eat only at specific mealtimes, not every time you have a craving.
2. Do not eat alone.
3. Remove unhealthy foods from the home.
4. If specific types of foods, such as sweets, are the focus of the addiction, limit the amount by having friends or family control the portions.
5. Learn how to manage your mood and stress levels, which are often triggers for overeating.
6. Start fun and healthy behaviors, such as exercise or a craft, to replace the overconsumption of food.

Key Points for Family Members

1. Family members should model healthy eating behaviors by exhibiting portion control and not eating between meals.
2. Family members should take control of cooking to control unhealthy ingredients in prepared dishes.
3. Family should encourage other sources of fun, including exercise and socializing.

8

Shopping and Buying

Diane is 38 years old and has two children in elementary school. She and her husband have full-time careers they love. Working downtown, Diane often meets colleagues from her office at a shopping mall for lunch. After lunch, she spends a little time looking through the shops before going back to work.

Diane got a huge promotion about six months ago, and since then she has felt her levels of stress going up and up. Because she has a managerial position now, with authority over people who used to be her peers, she more often goes to lunch by herself instead of with her colleagues. And she has switched from window shopping after lunch to actually making purchases. "I felt great about the compliments I received from strangers walking back to work when I had something new, like a purse. It made me feel good about myself, and it temporarily relieved my stress."

Diane started buying more and more items each week. With more stress at the office and less time to shop in stores, she started shopping online when she got home after work, and even in her office at work. Spending thousands of dollars each week and knowing that her husband would object if he knew the extent of her shopping, Diane had her purchases shipped to a post office box close to work so her husband would not find out.

Diane's credit card bills started to mount along with her anxiety over a "need" to buy more and more. "Every new item I bought made me feel good but stressed at the same time, knowing that I was already in debt. I justified it by saying to myself, 'This new suit will pay for itself with the promotion I'll get by impressing my superiors.'" After a while, Diane reported, "I didn't even care about what I was buying. I just *needed* to go shopping and buy something." After about a year of many, many purchases, Diane felt more anxious and could no longer hide the financial difficulties, because creditors were calling her at home. Diane finally told her husband that she needed help—albeit for her mood, not for a shopping problem.

Why is it a problem if a person shops too much?

In the United States, an estimated 18 million people have compulsive buying disorder. We know that compulsive buying hurts people by causing mental health problems, financial difficulties, and marital discord. Compulsive buying appears to be similar to other addictions, where people report an inability to stop or inhibit their behaviors. Further, research indicates that compulsive buying generally follows a chronic course, meaning that without intervention, most individuals will continue engaging in the behavior and suffering the consequences.

People with compulsive buying have higher rates of default on their credit cards than other people and often have significant mental health problems resulting from the stress and anxiety of unpaid debts and the inability to curb their behavior. Such consequences affect everyone in society through higher credit interest rates and potentially more use of health care services to treat secondary depression or other health problems that can coincide with compulsive buying. People with this problem may continue to spiral downward into more and more debt, resulting in significant financial problems, including default or bankruptcy, which, again, adversely affects all consumers.

What are the differences between spending too much and compulsive buying disorder?

Shopping is a commonplace and culturally accepted activity, especially in Western society, and frequent shopping and the overacquisition of goods has a rich history. Historically and evolutionarily speaking, the acquisition of goods was considered useful for survival. Early societies would encourage the acquisition of goods and the hoarding of those goods to make life easier and increase the chances of survival. Possessions were a symbol of wealth and, more important, security.

Within American culture, one of the most prominent early examples of compulsive buying was Mary Todd Lincoln, wife to President Abraham Lincoln. She was known to go on shopping binges; for example, she once purchased eighty-four pairs of gloves from a department store, spent more than six hundred dollars (a huge sum in the mid-1800s) on curtains that she had no use for, and bought several watches, seven hundred dollars in jewelry, and hundreds of dollars' worth of perfumes and soaps. Today's compulsive shoppers also go on shopping binges of comparable magnitude and buy items they have no use for. An important note, however, is that Mrs. Lincoln may have suffered from bipolar disorder; the similarities and differences between bipolar disorder and compulsive buying disorder are discussed later in this chapter.

As illustrated by the case of Mary Todd Lincoln, compulsive buying is, at its core, a disorder of acquisition. Research into compulsive buying has generally been limited to Western nations, including the United States, the United Kingdom, Germany, and Austria, where shopping (and overconsumption) is even marketed as a means of relieving stress or feeling better about oneself (for example, "I need retail therapy" or "When times get tough, the tough go shopping"). It should come as no surprise in such cultures of consumption that some individuals will overindulge in compulsive spending. Though most shoppers have no major problem inhibiting their impulses to shop, a small percentage develop a shopping addiction. Other potentially addictive behaviors, such as drinking alcohol, are also marketed to the Western public, reflecting the cultural complexities associated with compulsive shopping. For example, a common suggestion in Western countries is "Have a drink. It'll calm your nerves." Similar to those who drink too much and become alcoholics, a small percentage of individuals find their shopping behaviors extremely hard to control, and their shopping significantly affects their health and well-being. These are individuals with compulsive buying disorder.

With nearly all research on compulsive buying conducted in Western societies, critics of the disorder question whether it is a "real" disorder, since cultures in which shopping is not a commonplace activity lack reports of individuals with disordered shopping. After all, without access to shopping, one cannot have a compulsive buying problem. This reasoning makes critics question the biological basis of the disease. They contend that categorizing compulsive buying as a "disorder" is simply the "medicalization" of a behavioral problem.

Is compulsive buying disorder a formal disorder?

Neither of the two widely used catalogs of mental health problems—the tenth edition of the *International Classification of Diseases* (ICD-10), published by the World Health Organization (WHO), and the fifth edition of the *Diagnostic and Statistical Manual of Mental Disorders* (DSM-5), published by the American Psychiatric Association—recognizes compulsive buying as a mental health problem. For many people, this lack of recognition makes their struggles feel illegitimate, as if they are simply making it all up. In addition, popular culture tends to trivialize the behavior; bumper stickers encourage people to "Honk if you're a shopaholic," and movies and television make excessive shopping seem like a funny badge of honor for wealthy adolescent females and young socialites. Even though compulsive buying has not been recognized as a mental health problem, it has been discussed seriously by mental health professionals for the last one hundred years.

Some researchers suggest that compulsive buying is defined by four stages: anticipation, preparation, shopping, and spending. These stages appear to be cyclical, with many individuals reporting that an anticipatory urge to shop is "completed" after the act of purchasing. In fact, studies have shown that about half of patients with compulsive buying report irresistible urges, uncontrolled needs, or a sense of mounting tension relieved only by shopping. As Diane reported, "I would think about and plan my shopping in the morning while in meetings at work and get more and more excited as the lunch hour drew near. After finally being able to purchase new items during lunch, I often returned to my office feeling relieved. It was like a weight was lifted from my shoulders, but I knew the urge would likely come back the next morning."

Although formalized criteria for compulsive buying disorder have yet to be established, criteria have been proposed that validate the stages described by researchers and by Diane:

1. Maladaptive preoccupation with or engagement in buying as evidenced by frequent and irresistible impulses to buy, frequent buying of items that are not needed or not affordable, or shopping for longer periods than initially intended
2. Preoccupation with shopping or the buying itself that leads to significant distress or impairment
3. Buying that does not occur exclusively during manic episodes (as seen in bipolar disorder) or primarily when under the influence of substances

Clinical aspects of compulsive buying

How do I know if my shopping is a disorder?

This is not always an easy question to answer, particularly in Western societies, where shopping is a part of the culture, and overspending is common. One must remember that someone who shops regularly does not necessarily have a compulsive buying *disorder*. For example, people often overshop or overspend during the holiday season and feel guilty about it afterward. Does this mean that the person has a compulsive buying disorder? Not necessarily. An individual's motivation to shop, the degree of distress over the time or money spent, consequences resulting from the shopping, and the degree of control over the behavior can all help to distinguish compulsive buying from potentially problematic buying behaviors. To understand when too much shopping equals a disorder, we must understand what other problems may result in compulsive shopping and spending.

How do I know it is compulsive buying and not something else?

Depression

Depressive symptoms are extremely common in people with a compulsive buying disorder. Samples of people who have this disorder indicate that anywhere from 1 in 5 (20 percent) to all patients with compulsive buying disorder have a co-occurring mood disorder. Though this comorbidity is common, depression and compulsive buying are two different disorders and should be differentiated from each other. Patients often report that their shopping binges or overacquisition of items started shortly after they began feeling depressed. Properly identifying the order of occurrence can help in determining whether the depression prompted the compulsive buying disorder or whether the buying resulted in the patient feeling depressed. "I felt down every day, not feeling good about myself, so I went to the mall. Buying new clothes really lifted my mood, so I found myself going back daily to buy more and more. Now I feel depressed and stressed from the debt I have, but I still shop. If I see a sale, I have to take advantage!" In this person's case, the depression appears to predate the compulsive buying problem, but the excessive buying and subsequent development of compulsive buying disorder in turn made the depressive symptoms worse. Deciding whether the behavior (compulsive shopping) or the mood disorder (depression) came first, if possible, can help focus treatment in the right direction.

Bipolar disorder

The possibility of bipolar disorder must be considered by health care professionals when screening someone for a compulsive buying disorder. A manic episode is the defining feature of bipolar disorder (also referred to as manic depressive illness). In manic states, people often exhibit high levels of grandiosity (or extreme irritability), impulsive behaviors such as overspending, not sleeping, and unrealistic planning tendencies. The main difference between bipolar and compulsive buying is in the duration of shopping and spending symptoms as well as the narrower and more restricted range of symptoms seen with compulsive buying.

When people with bipolar disorder are in a manic state, they may have shopping "episodes" in which they spend large amounts of money, which often resembles the uncontrolled spending seen in compulsive buying disorder. But they are also likely to engage in multiple other forms of impulsive behavior, such as setting up bizarre new businesses, having too much sex, and feeling so full of energy they do not sleep. Patients with compulsive buying disorder report a more consistent, longer-term ongoing problem and preoccupation with spending that bipolar patients generally will not experience once the manic episode has remitted. The distinction between bipolar disorder and compulsive buying is important because the treatments and management approaches are very different for these two disorders.

Hoarding disorder

It is common for individuals with a compulsive buying problem to acquire a large amount of goods, much of which remains unused. For example, Diane reported, "I had so many purses and suits with the price tags still on them that I didn't know what to do with them. I had piles of unused clothes in the basement at my home—so much that it was hard to walk down there." Hoarding is characterized by behavior in which the individual collects items—often in groupings of the same or similar items. Those with a hoarding disorder, however, experience extreme anxiety when confronted with the prospect of discarding items or decluttering their home, whereas those with a compulsive buying problem generally lack such anxiety. Further, the motivation to collect items in hoarding disorder is generally driven by *catastrophizing*—obsessing over bad things happening if the person discards an item or does not obtain more things. "I cannot get rid of those eighty cups because what if I have a party and don't have enough cups for everyone? That would be embarrassing, and my friends and family would hate me." While hoarding behaviors can occur and are somewhat common in compulsive buying, such catastrophizing is relatively rare among people with compulsive buying disorder.

Consequences of compulsive buying

Financial

The most obvious consequence of compulsive buying is financial difficulties. Credit card debt, overdrawn bank accounts, and bankruptcy are all common in those with compulsive buying disorder. Financial burdens can create other problems, including knock-on mental health issues, occupational consequences, and family problems. Debt may be the trigger that motivates someone to seek help for compulsive buying. In one study, more than half of the participants reported that large debts or the inability to pay off debts was a trigger for them to seek help.

Mental health

Co-occurring (or comorbid) mental health problems are the norm rather than the exception for those with a compulsive buying disorder. The question of whether such problems usually predate the compulsive buying problem or result from the compulsive shopping has yet to be established. The health care provider should assess depressive symptoms, anxiety, and alcohol and drug use to determine which of the comorbid problems occurred first. This can be important from a treatment perspective: failing to recognize co-occurring disorders may result in the treatment being less effective. Therefore, patients and their family members need to let health care providers know what other problems the person may have struggled with in the past or is currently struggling with.

Family and social life

Many people with compulsive buying disorder have marital dysfunction and social problems. Approximately half of those with compulsive buying disorder report marital problems or family problems stemming from their compulsive buying. Shame, embarrassment, guilt, and other emotions cause many people with compulsive buying disorder to go to great lengths to conceal the amount of material purchased and debts incurred from their compulsive spending. Diane reported, "I wanted to make sure my husband did not find out about all the things I was buying. I knew he would be upset, and the sad realization hit me in treatment that I was more concerned about his finding out and stopping me from shopping than I was about how it would affect our marriage."

How common is compulsive buying?

A recent survey of 2,513 adults in the United States found that 5.8 percent (more than 1 in 20 people) had a shopping problem consistent with compulsive buying disorder. The prevalence of the disorder likely varies by country, based on wealth and on the availability and acceptance of shopping. Research in nonwesternized cultures has not been conducted, and therefore we simply do not know whether compulsive buying disorder is prevalent in societies in which shopping is not as common or accepted.

Is compulsive buying disorder a female problem?

Although early research indicated that compulsive buying was seen primarily among women, later studies reveal that a fairly substantial proportion of men may also have compulsive buying disorder. For example, the study of 2,513 adults noted above found a fairly equal percentage of men and women among those who had a compulsive buying problem. Similar results were noted in a German survey of 2,530 adults, where nearly equal percentages of men (6.8 percent) and women (6.9 percent) screened positive for compulsive buying. Women, however, are generally more interested in seeking help for their problem. This fact is certainly not unique to compulsive buying or, quite frankly, most other mental health and medical conditions. Men seek clinical care far less often than women for mental health problems. Family members, therefore, may need to nudge men with compulsive buying to seek treatment.

When does compulsive buying start?

Compulsive buying symptoms generally start in the late teens to early twenties, yet some studies have shown onset of disordered shopping around 30 years of age as well. For most people with compulsive buying disorder, the problem starts in their late teens, but the majority do not realize that they have a problem until much later in life—sometimes a decade or more from onset to realization. Guilt, legal problems, such as bankruptcy, and the inability to control debt can lead to this awareness. Once compulsive buying starts, however, it appears to follow a chronic course and usually does not simply stop on its own.

Why does someone develop compulsive buying disorder?

The answer to this question is unclear at this time. No one truly understands why someone develops a compulsive shopping problem. One theory suggests that early childhood abuse or neglect propagates the behavior later in life as a means of coping in adulthood. Psychoanalytic theories of early childhood sexual abuse in those with compulsive buying disorder have not been scientifically validated. Another theory suggests that financial emancipation from family in the late teens and early twenties, when teenagers often leave the nest and gain access to credit, may promote the development of compulsive buying. If it were simply due to this change in circumstances, however, everyone would develop a compulsive buying problem, and we know that is not the case. Therefore, it may be that these individuals are "primed" to develop an addiction such as compulsive buying and simply gain the means (credit) to engage in the behavior at a given age.

Research in other addictions has found that individuals with a family history of other addictive behaviors such as alcohol abuse or smoking are more likely to develop an addiction themselves. This may suggest a familial component to compulsive buying behavior, although the association between genetic factors (family heritability) and environmental factors (credit, access to shopping) is poorly understood at this time.

The biology of compulsive buying disorder

One theory about the role of biology in this behavior is that areas of the brain known to be involved in impulse control (the ability to stop oneself from engaging in a behavior) may be different in people with compulsive buying than in other people. Perhaps this suggests problems with the dopamine or opioid systems in the brain, areas that are heavily implicated in addictive behaviors and impulse control.

Other research suggests strong similarities between the repetitive nature of compulsive shopping and obsessive-compulsive disorder (OCD). Briefly, OCD is characterized by intrusive recurrent obsessive thoughts that increase anxiety (obsessions) or repetitive behaviors or mental acts (compulsions) that are done as a consequence of an obsession and that aim to decrease anxiety or that are undertaken according to rigid rules. The symptoms of compulsive buying often mimic such obsessive thoughts (for example, "I need to buy more purses to feel better") and compulsive behaviors (for example, buying purses). This link between behavior and symptoms of OCD would suggest there are problems with a neurotransmitter in the brain known as serotonin, which is recognized as being dysfunctional in the brains of people who have OCD.

Only one brain imaging study and three cognitive studies have been conducted examining neurobiological differences between those with a compulsive buying problem and those without. Neuroimaging studies allow us to see either the structure of the brain (the connectivity of the brain through *diffusion tensor imaging* [DTI]) or how much oxygen and blood are driven to certain parts of the brain when we make everyday decisions such as problem solving. The tests that show changes related to specific thoughts are called *functional* magnetic resonance imaging, or fMRI. There are numerous other techniques to study the brain, but DTI and fMRI are the most common in mental health research. Studies of cognition help us to understand how certain areas of the brain respond when presented with an everyday task. For example, we know that certain areas of the brain are responsible for our ability to inhibit a behavior ("Those shoes are fantastic, but I have to wait until I get paid before I buy them"). For those with an addictive behavior such as compulsive buying, it is thought that parts of the brain responsible for such inhibitory control may be different from those in people who do not have a shopping problem.

The only neuroimaging study conducted so far compared twenty-three compulsive buyers with twenty-six people who did not have compulsive buying, all of whom were women. All participants underwent brain imaging with fMRI. The hypothesis was that the striatal area of the brain (part of the reward and motivation center), including the nucleus accumbens, would show abnormalities when compulsive buyers performed a task of looking at different products, seeing the price of those products, and ultimately making a decision to purchase those products, compared with no abnormalities in the brains of women without compulsive buying disorder. As noted elsewhere in this book, these parts of the brain are known to be involved in reward processing and have been shown to be dysfunctional in individuals with other addictions. As expected, compulsive buyers exhibited a more active nucleus accumbens (meaning greater urges and motivation) when viewing products and a less active insula (meaning less self-awareness and less motor control) when viewing both product and price. The results provide biological support for the loss of control over their shopping behaviors reported by those with compulsive buying disorder.

Cognitive research has also shed light on what may be happening in the brains of those with compulsive buying disorder. Although one study failed to find any differences between compulsive buyers and healthy controls, the other two studies have found differences. On computerized cognitive tasks, those with compulsive buying disorder exhibit significant impairments in inhibitory control, the ability to accurately assess risk during decision making, and working memory. The results suggest significant similarities between people with compulsive buying disorder and those with other behavioral and substance addictions.

How is compulsive buying treated?

Our knowledge of effective psychological and medication treatments for compulsive buying disorder is quite limited at this time. As noted earlier, most individuals with a compulsive buying problem do not seek treatment for several reasons, including shame or embarrassment and a belief that compulsive buying disorder is nothing more than a bad habit.

Certain therapies and medications that have proven effective for other mental health problems, such as addiction and obsessive-compulsive disorder, have shown some promise in treating the symptoms of compulsive buying disorder.

Therapy

One of the most common and effective therapies used in mental health conditions, including addictions, is called cognitive behavioral therapy, or CBT. As the name implies, CBT focuses both on individuals' cognitive processing and on their behavior. Cognitive processes include how people think through problems, how they think about their behavior, and what thoughts precede and follow a behavior. Behaviors are defined as what individuals are doing and when as well as how often they engage in the behavior.

Group CBT has shown real promise in the treatment of compulsive buying. Usually therapy is done once weekly for ten to twelve weeks. The research shows that people in the therapy groups have reduced both the time spent shopping and the sheer number of buying episodes. In addition, the research on group CBT followed patients for six months after they completed the treatment, to see whether any gains made during the course of treatment were maintained. Encouragingly, all studies reported that patients continued to experience positive effects of their treatment at this follow-up.

In motivational interviewing and imaginal desensitization, an audio recording is made of an individual's "typical" compulsive shopping and buying episode. These techniques have been implemented successfully for patients with compulsive buying disorder. For imaginal desensitization, the individual first writes down in detail what happens prior to, during, and after a compulsive buying episode. Either the therapist or the patient then records an audio version of the written script, and the individual is instructed to listen to that recording several times each day during the course of therapy.

This description allows patients to imagine a typical episode of shopping, eliciting the same urges (prior to shopping), excitement (during the buying episode), and shame, embarrassment, and guilt (after the buying episode) that they would feel in an actual shopping episode, only this time in a controlled environment. A 27-year-old woman with compulsive buying disorder was treated with six sessions of one-hour CBT, including imaginal desensitization. After therapy, she reported that her urges to shop were significantly reduced, with improvement maintained for six months after treatment. She also reported using the recorded script when she had urges to shop to help her to realize that she had control over her shopping episodes and to maintain her improvements. This particular therapy has been shown to be helpful for other behavioral addictions, such as gambling addiction and kleptomania.

April Benson has developed a guided self-help program for compulsive buyers that can be used by individuals or groups. The program combines CBT strategies with other types of therapy (psychodynamic, acceptance and commitment). She also provides a detailed workbook with exercises, a shopping diary, and a CD-ROM with guided visualizations. Although the research on her program is limited, the overall approach appears to address the issues of compulsive buyers very appropriately.

Support groups

Patterned after Alcoholics Anonymous, Debtors Anonymous is available in many cities worldwide. The group provides an atmosphere of mutual support and encouragement. The members are people with substantial debts, and membership is not limited to compulsive buyers, although many members do have compulsive buying problems. Individuals participating in Debtors Anonymous get a sponsor and work through an approach based on the twelve steps of AA.

Medications

There is little evidence at this time for the treatment of compulsive buying disorder with medications. Currently, no medications are approved by regulatory boards for the treatment of compulsive buying disorder.

Antidepressants that affect the brain chemical serotonin have so far produced mixed results in treating people who have compulsive buying disorder. Although some people have benefited from these medications, antidepressants that affect serotonin have not shown substantial bene-fit in research studies when patients taking the medications are compared with patients taking placebos (sugar pills or other "pills" that contain no medication). Therefore, although they might help someone with compul-sive buying who also has significant depression or anxiety, they will likely be less helpful for the symptoms of compulsive buying itself.

Some research supports the use of naltrexone, which is FDA approved for alcoholism (50 mg to 100 mg per day), or memantine, which is FDA approved for Alzheimer's disease (10 mg to 20 mg per day), in treating compulsive buying. Individuals with compulsive buying, however, should understand that medication will not be a quick fix to their problem. Other aspects of the behavior need to be addressed in therapy.

Financial counseling

It is no surprise that financial problems are a hallmark of compulsive buy-ing disorder. Individuals and their family members should be aware of the stress that finances can place on all of them. Compulsive buyers and their family members should ask their health care professional for a re-ferral to available resources, such as trained financial counselors.

Transference of addiction

The financial problems—and subsequent stresses—experienced by people with a compulsive buying problem may, for some, lead to other po-tentially harmful behaviors, such as gambling, in a misguided attempt to "fix" their financial strains. Individuals and their family members must be aware of this possibility and take steps to guard against it. People with compulsive buying often "switch" to another addictive behavior during or soon after treatment for their compulsive buying. This is true for all addictions, as individuals struggle to replace the thrill or rush they re-ceived before undergoing treatment. When the compulsive buying is taken away, patients (often unconsciously) seek to replace the shopping with either a different behavior (for example, gambling) or a substance (for example, alcohol). Family members must be aware of this possibility and monitor the individual closely for symptoms of addiction transference.

Goals of treatment

Refraining from all shopping is not a realistic goal of treatment for most individuals who have a compulsive buying problem, unless the person is extremely wealthy or fortunate and can afford to have people do everything for them, including shopping. Furthermore, most individuals with a compulsive buying problem do not have compulsive spending issues in all facets of shopping (such as grocery shopping). During the acute phase of treatment, however, we strongly encourage people undergoing treatment to identify someone who (1) is aware of their struggles with compulsive shopping and (2) may be willing to help by doing their shopping for the time being.

Regardless of whether the person has an advocate who can help, an important aspect of treatment is encouraging people with compulsive buying disorder to make a list of specific items they absolutely need before going to the grocery store, mall, or anywhere else that offers the possibility of purchasing things. They must not deviate from the items on the list—easier said than done for many people with a compulsive buying problem.

What if treatment does not work?

Addictive behaviors such as compulsive buying are often difficult to treat. Furthermore, treatment failure and inadequate response to treatment are common. If treatment fails, the health care provider and the patient need to examine possible reasons for the treatment failure and reassess the situation before starting a new course of treatment. For example, does the person have adequate family or social supports? Research indicates that involving a support system, whether it be a family member, friend, or group setting such as Debtors Anonymous, can help the individual, especially in the early stages of treatment.

Case

Maryann is a 24-year-old woman with a college degree, a full-time job, and no children. She usually works at least sixty hours each week in an attorney's office as she tries to build her career.

In college, Maryann consumed alcohol every day: "Drinking was the culture at my school." After graduating, she drank twice a week, generally on weekends, and over the past couple of months, she increased her drinking to three, "sometimes four" days a week. On other nights, Maryann says she goes shopping at a mall on her way home from work. "Clothes and image are important to my job, so I don't think it's a problem that I buy new clothes a few days a week." She visits her doctor because, she says, "I don't have enough money to do things with my friends, and I'm starting to feel depressed."

Maryann struggles with alcohol abuse and mild depression. Closer inspection of her shopping indicates a significant compulsive buying problem. She has about ten thousand dollars in credit card debt from buying new clothes "a few days a week." She says, "My friends don't want to shop with me because they don't have as much money to spend."

Maryann is offered weekly therapy to address the cognitive distortions surrounding her shopping and to help her reduce her alcohol intake. Her cognitive distortions lead her to ignore the fact that people do not want to shop with her because they are uncomfortable with all the things she buys and all the money she spends. After ten sessions, Maryann begins to recognize that she is compensating for work stress with shopping binges and that she uses alcohol to "remove myself from the stress of my job and dwindling friendships." Maryann is encouraged to reach out to her friends, and she does. After ten weeks of weekly therapy, she reports that she has reduced both her shopping excursions and her alcohol intake to when she is on social outings with friends. Maryann has also connected with a financial counselor at the urging of her therapist and is working at rebuilding her credit. She reports feeling much more in control of her shopping and her financial situation and plans to continue meeting with her therapist every few months to check in on her progress.

Key Points for Individuals with Compulsive Buying

1. Stop shopping completely for a period or only shop with someone who knows you have a problem.
2. If you have to shop, make shopping lists and limit your time in stores.
3. Use only cash for shopping; no credit or debit cards.
4. Do not shop online, and block the sites where you previously shopped; remove credit card information stored in certain websites.
5. Learn how to manage your mood and stress levels because these are often triggers for shopping.
6. If hoarding has become a part of the buying, you need to clean out things at home. Get friends to help or hire a professional to help clear clutter if you need assistance.

Key Points for Family Members

1. Family members should model nonshopping behaviors to cope with stress, depressed mood, and boredom.
2. Family members should help block shopping sites on the Internet and remind the person of activities other than shopping that are fun and stress reducing.
3. Family members should consider taking control of finances, checkbooks, credit cards, and debit cards, with the affected individual's permission.
4. Family should encourage other sources of fun, exercise, and socializing to take the place of acquiring things.

9

Hair Pulling and Skin Picking

Serena is a 33-year-old single woman who owns her own business and describes pulling her hair out since the age of 14. "I remember I started by pulling my eyelashes and making a wish. There was something about it that just felt 'right,' and I couldn't stop after that. About six months later, I started pulling from my head as well. That led to a lot of problems in school, with kids noticing the bald spots and making fun of me. I have never really dated because of the pulling. I enjoy my life and have good friends, but I probably would have done a lot differently if I had felt more confident and better about my appearance." Serena had tried various "tricks" she found on the Internet to help her stop pulling her hair, such as wearing hats and gloves, but these methods had not helped.

Serena came for treatment for her hair pulling because she had read that there were physicians and therapists who treated this problem. She began weekly habit-reversal therapy and continued for six months. Although she still pulled occasionally, she was not doing it every day, and her hair had begun to regrow. "I never thought it was possible to have hair again. I feel like I have my life back."

Rita is a 24-year-old graduate student who is single and lives alone. She began picking at her face when she was about 10 years old. "I can't remember why I started doing it. I remember my mother yelling at me to stop picking, and she would slap my hands, but I kept doing it." Rita picks at her face daily, sometimes for an hour or more. Although she says she is picking at bumps and other things that "are wrong," it becomes clear that first she has a desire to pick, and then she scans her face to find an area to pick. The picking has scarred Rita's face, and when she initially came for treatment, she was bleeding from a few spots. She kept a cap pulled over her forehead and could not look her physician in the eyes because she was so embarrassed. "This has ruined my life. People think that I am a drug addict or that I have some serious disease. Either way, no one wants to know me. They stare and stare, so I stay at home and never go out except to attend class. I feel so lonely and depressed."

Rita began treatment with habit-reversal therapy. She also started N-acetylcysteine, an amino acid, to reduce her urges to pick. After approximately four months, Rita was able to go several days in a row without any picking. After ten months, Rita picked only once in a great while. Her face slowly started to heal. "I no longer hide from people. I can actually be in public and not feel embarrassed."

Why should anyone care about hair pulling and skin picking?

For many people who develop hair-pulling or skin-picking problems, the behavior is associated with impaired functioning, health problems (for example, infections), and reduced quality of life. These forms of dysfunctional grooming have been defined by the American Psychiatric Association in the fifth edition of the *Diagnostic and Statistical Manual of Mental Disorders* (*DSM-5*) as "Trichotillomania (Hair-Pulling Disorder)" and "Excoriation (Skin-Picking) Disorder."

Although hair pulling and skin picking are separate disorders, we have grouped them together for this chapter because they have many similarities and are examples of *overgrooming behaviors* that a person cannot control. Compulsive nail biting may be another example. Every person, and most animals, groom themselves. Pulling a single gray hair or picking a piece of skin off one's fingers is normal behavior. In fact, most people groom daily, without any significant consequences and with no difficulty controlling the behaviors. For some people, however, the ability to stop the grooming process is not sufficient and may continue even when nothing is realistically left to be groomed.

The idea of grooming behaviors becoming problems for some people is not new. Although incompletely understood, these behaviors have been recognized for hundreds of years by the medical community. Hippocrates, the father of Western medicine, who lived between the years 460 BC and 370 BC, described conditions that mirror today's trichotillomania and excoriation disorder. The English surgeon and dermatologist Erasmus Wilson, in 1875, first used the term *neurotic excoriation* to describe neurotic patients' excessive picking behaviors, which the patients found extremely difficult, if not impossible, to control. François Hallopeau, a French dermatologist, coined the term *trichotillomania* in 1889 to describe people who could not stop pulling their hair.

Trichotillomania was officially recognized by the American Psychiatric Association in 1987 as an impulse control disorder, and it remained in that section until 2013, when it was moved to the chapter in the *DSM-5* on "Obsessive Compulsive and Related Disorders." Excoriation disorder was only recognized as a legitimate mental health problem in 2013, and then, like trichotillomania, it was included in *DSM-5* in the category of disorders referred to as being related to obsessive-compulsive disorder (OCD). Although these behaviors have been grouped with OCD, they also seem to have much in common with substance addictions from the perspective of the person's inability to stop the behavior despite multiple problems, strong urges to do the behavior, and often a sense of pleasure from the picking and pulling. These similarities with addictions are why we have included skin picking and hair pulling in this book.

How are trichotillomania and excoriation disorder diagnosed?

There is no blood test or brain scan that can determine whether someone has trichotillomania or excoriation disorder. The diagnosis is made by what a person and the family tell the clinician. Family members and other loved ones can often provide valuable information that gives a clearer picture of the person's struggles with the behavior.

The essential feature of trichotillomania is recurrent pulling of hair that results in psychosocial dysfunction. To receive the diagnosis of trichotillomania, an individual must have the following symptoms:

1. The person pulls her hair on multiple occasions, and the pulling results in some hair loss.
2. The person has tried to decrease or stop hair pulling on at least a couple of occasions.
3. The person reports that the hair pulling causes her distress or that the pulling has resulted in problems socially, at work, or in another area of functioning.

Similarly, the essential feature of excoriation disorder is an inability to stop picking at one's skin. To receive the diagnosis of excoriation disorder, an individual must have the following symptoms:

1. The person picks his skin recurrently, and the picking results in skin lesions such as scarring or excoriations.
2. The person has tried to decrease or stop picking on at least a couple of occasions.
3. The person reports that the skin picking has caused distress or has resulted in problems with his ability to function well at work, at school, or socially.

Important clinical aspects of these behaviors

A physician or therapist who makes the diagnosis needs to do more than simply check off the symptoms and say "yes" or "no"—the person has or does not have trichotillomania or excoriation disorder. The health care provider's assessment of someone with one of these disorders focuses on the triggers to the behavior, what the person may derive from the behavior in both positive and negative ways, related mental and physical issues, previous treatments, what the person has tried on her own to control her behavior, and what the person currently expects from treatment. The evaluation also must include a detailed understanding of the extent of the hair pulling or skin picking (how often and how much), the repercussions of the problem on the individual's lifestyle (for example, social, psychological, and familial) and on her physical health (for example, infections or eating hair), the person's readiness for change, and her sense of control over the grooming behavior.

Anyone may develop trichotillomania or excoriation disorder. Both men and women can develop these problems, albeit most studies have found that both behaviors are more common in women.

Hair pulling generally begins in late childhood or early adolescence, although it can start at any age. Trichotillomania appears to occur in similar ways among people, even in different cultures. It is frequently associated with reduced self-esteem and avoidance of social situations because of shame and embarrassment from the pulling and its consequences. Even though trichotillomania interferes with a person's quality of life, the majority (about 65 percent) of individuals with trichotillomania never seek treatment.

The age when skin picking begins varies widely; it may occur during childhood, adolescence, or adulthood. The clinical characteristics of excoriation disorder appear the same in different age cohorts and cultures. Many individuals report that the behavior began with the onset of a dermatological condition such as acne, but the picking continues even after the dermatological condition clears.

Individuals with trichotillomania or excoriation disorder may spend a significant amount of time each day pulling their hair or picking their skin. The face is the most commonly reported site of picking and the head for pulling, although any area may be pulled or picked. Picking and pulling from more than one body area is common. Triggers for picking or pulling vary greatly between individuals, and multiple triggers are the norm. Triggers may be sensory (for example, hair thickness, skin texture), emotional (for example, feeling anxious), or cognitive (for example, thoughts about hair and skin appearance). Many patients report not being fully aware of their pulling or picking, in which case it is considered *automatic* behavior. By contrast, *focused* pulling or picking generally occurs when the person sees or feels a hair or part of the skin that is "not right." Most people pull or pick with varying degrees of focused and automatic behavior, which can fluctuate over time.

Consequences of hair pulling and skin picking

Both trichotillomania and excoriation disorder may result in unwanted medical consequences. Pulling of hair can lead to skin damage if sharp instruments, such as tweezers or scissors, are used to pull the hairs. Some people with trichotillomania eat hair after pulling it out; this condition is called *trichophagia*—a habit that can lead to gastrointestinal obstruction caused by intestinal hair balls (*trichobezoars*) that form from the swallowed hair. Surgery is sometimes necessary in order to remove the hair balls. In skin picking, the behavior may result in significant tissue damage and often leads to medical complications, such as localized infections and even septicemia.

Excoriation disorder and trichotillomania may also lead to other mental health problems. One study found that many individuals with excoriation disorder used illegal drugs or alcohol to relieve feelings associated with the physical and emotional consequences of skin picking. In addition, many people with trichotillomania or excoriation disorder report social anxiety and depression as a result of their behaviors.

How common are trichotillomania and excoriation disorder?

National epidemiological studies of trichotillomania and excoriation disorder have not yet been done. Small studies examining the prevalence of trichotillomania among college students in the United States, adolescents in Israel, and older adults within the general population have found current rates ranging from 0.5 to 2 percent. College and community prevalence studies in the United States, Germany, and Israel have found that excoriation disorder is also relatively common, with prevalence rates ranging from 1.4 to 5.4 percent.

Are hair pulling and skin picking always mental health disorders?

Excessive grooming can occur when a person is using or misusing stimulant medications or drugs. It is not uncommon for individuals who use stimulants, either illicit or prescription, to report worsening of their hair pulling or skin picking in response to skin sensations resulting from drug use. Stimulant use often makes an existing hair-pulling or skin-picking problem worse. To find out whether the person has a pulling or picking problem that is not related to stimulant use, the physician or therapist will ask about any use of stimulants and will encourage individuals to discuss any such use openly and honestly. Patients are more comfortable sharing this information if health care providers inform them that they do not have a legal duty to report the use of illicit substances and reassure them that they will not do so.

Stimulants may worsen or possibly even cause picking and pulling behaviors, and therefore people should assess how much caffeine they are drinking or eating each day. Large doses of caffeine may also result in these problems.

Hair pulling and skin picking are also possible symptoms of body dysmorphic disorder (BDD). BDD is characterized by obsessions about and preoccupation with a perceived defect of one's physical features. Individuals with BDD might obsess over perceived skin blemishes and pick at those areas, or might pull hair with the aim of correcting a perceived defect in their appearance (for example, "I think my eyebrows are bushy and disgusting"). If the behaviors are performed because a person is concerned about the appearance of some part or parts of her body that she considers particularly unattractive, and if the concerns preoccupy the person, then BDD is a more appropriate diagnosis than trichotillomania or excoriation disorder.

Sometimes a person with obsessive-compulsive disorder (OCD) will pick at skin and pull hair, although this behavior is fairly rare in OCD. In these cases, someone may pick to remove contaminants from the skin, and the picking is essentially a compulsion driven by contamination obsessions. Similarly, hair pulling may occur as part of obsessions about symmetry. For these people, the pulling and picking are considered a symptom of OCD, and OCD is the focus of treatment.

Individuals suffering from some psychotic disorders, including a delusion that they are infested with parasites (*parasitosis*), may pick at their skin. These individuals are convinced that there is something under their skin, including bugs or an "infestation," that they must uncover and rid the body of.

Why does someone develop trichotillomania or excoriation disorder?

Family and genetic influences

Research on family history suggests that excoriation and trichotillomania are often familial; that is, they tend to run in families. One study found that about one-third of people with skin-picking disorder had a first-degree family member (parent, child, or sibling) who also had excoriation disorder. When individuals with excoriation disorder were compared with those who had OCD, it was found that people with skin picking had higher rates of co-occurring compulsive nail biting and were more likely to have a first-degree relative with a grooming disorder. A study from the United Kingdom found that skin picking was more common in identical twins than in fraternal twins, indicating that there is a strong genetic influence on skin picking. Similar findings have been reported in trichotillomania. In addition, individuals with trichotillomania are more likely to have a family member with a substance addiction (21.6 percent alcohol addiction and 14.7 percent drug addiction) than relatives of people without these conditions. These findings suggest that if you have a first-degree relative with one of these problems, you are much more likely to have it yourself. Thus, skin picking, hair pulling, and substance addictions, at least in some people, may share an underlying genetic vulnerability, and a person with this genetic predisposition may be more likely to develop one of these behaviors.

We also have learned about the genetics of grooming from research on animals. Hair pulling and skin picking are behaviors that are also seen in animals, and some animals are not able to stop their grooming behaviors, just as some humans cannot. Animal research on the gene encoding SAPAP3, a protein found in excitatory glutamate-responsive synapses, which are largely in the part of the brain known as the striatum (the part involved in reward and motivation), led to research in humans. In humans, this gene was found to be associated with human excoriation disorder. In addition, the particular variant of the SAPAP3 gene found in excoriation was not associated with OCD. This lends further support to the idea that these grooming disorders are not the same as OCD and probably should not be treated similarly.

Another important finding from animal research has been the Hoxb8 gene, which appears to play a role in grooming. Mice with mutations of the Hoxb8 gene groom excessively, so much so that they develop skin lesions. The excessive grooming of animals with Hoxb8 gene mutations is similar to the excessive grooming seen in humans with excoriation disorder or trichotillomania. What this finding may tell us about human hair-pulling and skin-picking disorders is not yet clear.

The brain

Cognitive research has attempted to explain both cognitive and biological processes involved in trichotillomania and excoriation disorder. The repetitive physical symptoms of pulling and picking suggest underlying dysfunction of the control processes of our brain that tell us to stop behaviors. Being able to inhibit one's response to such tasks is dependent on brain circuitry that includes the front area of the brain (including the right inferior frontal gyrus). Individuals with skin picking or hair pulling have impairments in inhibiting their behavior. Even the first-degree relatives of people with trichotillomania appear to have this same problem with inhibiting their behavior, which suggests that the cognitive dysfunction underlying these behaviors runs in families, and that the cognitive dysfunction may predate the onset of the behavior.

Several brain structures and functions have been studied for their possible involvement in trichotillomania and excoriation disorder. People with hair-pulling or skin-picking disorder show differences in both gray and white matter in brain areas that are involved in the ability to start and stop movements. (Gray matter is associated with cognition, and white matter coordinates communication between different brain regions. Gray matter and white matter are two major components of the central nervous system.)

Treatment of trichotillomania and excoriation disorder

Even though trichotillomania and excoriation disorder negatively affect a person's quality of life, only a small proportion of the individuals who are suffering from these behaviors seek or receive formal treatment, in part because most people with these disorders do not know that their "habit" is a mental health problem with available treatments. This may be particularly true in the case of excoriation disorder, which was only recognized as a mental health disorder in 2013. Research indicates that fewer than 20 percent of subjects seek treatment for their picking (a generous estimate, in our opinion), and that individuals with skin picking often report that they were not aware that viable treatments were available. Moreover, many of our patients report that they told their doctor about their hair pulling or skin picking and were prescribed inappropriate treatments or told that treatments were not available. Physicians need to become more aware of these disorders, and individuals who have these disorders need to mention the behavior to their physicians and ask for appropriate treatment.

What happens if the person does not receive treatment?

If trichotillomania and excoriation disorder are not treated, the disorders usually become chronic, often with waxing and waning symptoms. Without treatment, recovery rates in adults are low (approximately 14 percent). When people are diagnosed early and are appropriately treated, however, up to 50 percent of individuals experience reduction in their symptoms, at least for the short term. Accurate and early diagnosis followed by evidence-based treatment approaches are therefore needed to prevent associated disability.

The importance of proper diagnosis and appropriate treatment

Misdiagnosis of trichotillomania and excoriation disorder is unfortunately common. Individuals may be misdiagnosed with obsessive-compulsive disorder (OCD), another anxiety disorder, or even a drug addiction. Although the repetitive motor symptoms of hair pulling and skin picking resemble compulsive rituals in OCD, individuals with trichotillomania or excoriation disorder are less likely to report obsessive thoughts and may not even be aware of their behavior if it happens automatically. In addition, individuals with excessive grooming disorders may be more impulsive than people with OCD and may demonstrate little if any response to treatment with selective serotonin reuptake inhibitors (SSRIs). Importantly, the treatments used for OCD are different from the treatments recommended for trichotillomania and excoriation disorder. Therefore, proper diagnosis is critical.

The need for a physical examination

To be properly evaluated, individuals with trichotillomania or excoriation disorder may need a physical examination as well as a mental health assessment. Many individuals who are ashamed of their behavior do not admit how persistent it is. But often, people with these disorders have significant skin injury with infections that need treatment, which can only be offered if the problems are revealed or identified. And although 10 to 15 percent of people with trichotillomania eat their hair, many of them are very ashamed to discuss this habit, and most of them do not initially admit to this behavior. If an individual with trichotillomania who eats her hair experiences abdominal pain or other signs of abdominal disease, careful physical examination is needed, in case the symptoms are due to a hair ball, which can lead to gastrointestinal obstruction—a potentially life-threatening condition.

The physical examination in excoriation disorder serves two purposes: first, to assess the magnitude of the picking and to develop appropriate interventions based on the damage to the skin; and second, to assess for possible dermatological or infectious causes for the skin picking. Many dermatological conditions cause people to scratch or pick—for example, scabies, atopic dermatitis, psoriasis, and blistering skin disorders. If a health care provider suspects that the patient has any of these conditions, a referral for a thorough dermatological consultation is recommended.

If a person is swallowing hair, she should be examined by a pediatrician or family doctor. The doctor may do both laboratory testing (blood work) and a CT scan of the abdomen to determine if a blockage is present. During the CT exam, the doctor will also check the abdomen for the mass of a hair ball; about 97 percent of trichobezoars are revealed during a CT scan examination. A child with an intestinal blockage caused by ingested hair should have an imaging exam twice each year to make sure that no further blockage occurs. If the child is no longer pulling hair after one year of follow-up, the imaging exams can be discontinued. If a blockage is discovered, surgery may be necessary to remove large trichobezoars. This surgery has a success rate of 99 percent.

Psychotherapy

Habit-reversal therapy

Habit-reversal therapy was first developed about forty years ago for the treatment of nervous habits and tics. Used in multiple forms throughout the years, the core aspects of HRT include self-monitoring (asking the patient to track his hair pulling, picking, and so on), awareness training, competing response training, and stimulus control procedures (such as modifying the environment to reduce cues for hair pulling or skin picking). *Self-monitoring* may begin by using a self-monitoring form that the patient fills out daily and maintains throughout the therapy period. *Awareness training* consists of having the therapist ask the patient to describe in detail and even reenact the picking or pulling. The patient also needs to identify triggers for the pulling and picking.

In *competing response training*, patients are taught—at the earliest sign of pulling, or any sign of the urge to pull—to engage in a behavior that is physically incompatible with pulling for a brief time, until the urge subsides. For example, someone who pulls her hair might clench her fists or place her hands underneath her legs when she identifies a warning sign for hair pulling. Competing responses must be opposite to that of the targeted behavior; they must be maintained for one minute or until the urge to pull or pick subsides; and they should be socially inconspicuous. *Stimulus control* consists of modifying the environment to reduce the triggers of pulling or picking. For example, if someone pulls at work only when the office door is closed, then she needs to keep the door open during the workday.

HRT can be delivered in person, online using a self-help method, or in a group format. Benefit obtained from HRT has generally been maintained for three to six months. Typically HRT is conducted weekly, although for severe behavior, the person may need more frequent sessions. HRT has shown benefit in many different frequency formats, and some number between four and twenty-two sessions (usually sixty minutes each) may be helpful. Although many clinicians use a combination of HRT and more traditional cognitive therapy, the empirical data support HRT as the first-line psychotherapy treatment for these behaviors.

Augmenting HRT with other therapies

Therapy is often enhanced when habit-reversal therapy is augmented with components of acceptance and commitment therapy and dialectical behavior therapy. *Acceptance and commitment therapy* (ACT) is a technique in which patients are asked to experience urges to pull or pick and to accept the urge without acting on it. The negative emotions involved with pulling or picking are also engaged but not acted on. The idea is that if people understand, feel, and experience that they do not have to respond to an urge or emotion, they are more able to feel in control of their pulling or picking.

Dialectical behavior therapy (DBT) has some similarities to ACT, including an emphasis on accepting uncomfortable internal experiences in combination with life change. DBT focuses on emotion regulation and distress tolerance, teaching skills to regulate emotion without pulling or picking. *Stress reduction training* may also be useful for individuals with trichotillomania or excoriation and should be used in conjunction with HRT or ACT. Depending on the person's triggers, learning how to reduce stress may further alleviate some of the intensity of pulling or picking urges and behavior.

Medications

No medication has received regulatory approval as a treatment for trichotillomania or excoriation disorder, but various pharmacological agents (glutamate agents and antipsychotics) have demonstrated some benefit in the treatment of these behaviors. These medications are often useful, but they are not magic pills for skin picking and hair pulling. Currently, no medications are universally accepted as first-line treatments for trichotillomania or excoriation disorder. Generally, pharmacotherapy should be avoided in children unless therapy has produced little or no benefit.

Medications that affect the chemical glutamate have shown some promise in helping people who have trichotillomania and excoriation disorder. One example is the nutritional supplement N-acetylcysteine (NAC), which has shown benefit for cocaine and marijuana addiction. NAC is purchased over the counter, usually from health food stores, vitamin shops, or online merchants. It is generally sold as an antioxidant or a supplement to enhance a person's immune system. NAC may be useful for reducing the urge to pick or pull in adults. Previous research has used up to 1200 mg twice a day as a target dose, with expected clinical benefits being observed after approximately nine weeks. Side effects are generally mild and usually involve only some bloated feelings, mild nausea, and flatulence. One problem with NAC is that there are questions of quality control—questions about "Which brand should I buy?" and "Are all brands equally effective?" The nutritional supplement world is generally unregulated, so it is not possible to recommend one brand over another with any real confidence. In children the use of NAC may be less promising. We are unclear why this would be the case. Having said that, we often recommend it to children or adolescents because it may help, and we have little else to offer in terms of medications.

Antipsychotic medications have also been used to treat trichotillomania and excoriation disorder. Low to moderate doses of olanzapine or aripiprazole (5 to 10 mg per day) have demonstrated benefit in reducing the symptoms of trichotillomania in adults after two to three months of taking the medications. These antipsychotic medications, however, have been associated with metabolic syndrome, so the decision to use them for treating trichotillomania or excoriation disorder needs to be tempered by their significant adverse side effect profile (aripiprazole has less severe side effects than olanzapine). Low doses of these medications appear generally safe in children and adolescents, but we prefer to see what therapy does before using these medications.

Opioid antagonists (for example, naltrexone) are FDA approved for alcoholism and have shown benefit in reducing excessive self-licking in dogs (a potential "animal model" of excessive grooming). They may also be a viable option for some adults with trichotillomania or excoriation disorder. Recent research showed that naltrexone may be beneficial in those with a pulling or picking behavior who also have a family history of alcoholism.

Many physicians over the years have recommended inositol, a B-vitamin complex, for people with trichotillomania. Although it showed excellent results in some people when used with therapy, we do not know how good it is or whom it is best for. We are currently conducting a study to answer these questions. Having said that, inositol is quite safe and is well tolerated. It is sprinkled as a powder (up to 6 grams three times per day) into food or beverages for several weeks.

Finally, many people with hair pulling or skin picking are put on antidepressants by their family doctor, who assumes the behaviors are a reflection of anxiety or are a form of OCD. There is no strong evidence of a treatment effect for the SSRIs, although some evidence suggests they may be slightly better for individuals with skin picking than for those with hair pulling. These medications may improve anxiety, and a reduction in anxiety in turn reduces, to some extent, the pulling or picking, but there is no good evidence that SSRIs work directly on changing the behavior. There are data supporting clomipramine, an older antidepressant, for treating these behaviors, and this medication should be considered when trichotillomania or excoriation disorder are also associated with significant depression or anxiety. Clomipramine is often used in children as well as adults, but the possible side effects often make it intolerable regardless of age (nausea, sweating, dry mouth, sexual side effects, constipation).

Based on all the published research, NAC or olanzapine appear to be the most promising medications for trichotillomania and excoriation, at least in adults. Because not everyone will benefit from these medications, and because of the side effects of olanzapine, other options are needed. A medication should be chosen based on several factors, including whether the patient has co-occurring disorders and what the patient's history tells us. Clomipramine may be the choice if the patient has co-occurring depression or anxiety. Naltrexone may be the choice for someone with a personal or family history of addictions. Inositol may also be a valuable option, although it is simply too early to tell.

How long does a person have to take medication?

If someone has found a medication helpful, we recommend that the person stay on the medication for at least one year. If the person's symptoms worsen after stopping the medication, it can be restarted and again given for another year.

Can a person receive therapy and medication together?

In our clinic, we find that therapy plus medication produces the best results for most people. No data suggest that receiving both together in any way makes one of them less effective.

Special issues in treatment

To choose the appropriate treatment for someone with trichotillomania or excoriation disorder, health care providers consider several factors related to medication and therapy:

1. Clinical treatment trials for trichotillomania and excoriation disorder have been largely short term and have predominantly involved young or middle-aged adults. The data support the use of habit-reversal therapy in children with hair-pulling or skin-

picking disorder, but there are no data to guide treatments regarding medications in younger people. Medication may be considered when therapy is largely ineffective, and the young person is suffering socially due to the pulling or picking. In those cases, clomipramine may be used, as it is FDA approved for children with OCD. NAC may also be worth a trial, although one study mimicking the protocol for the earlier adult study found that it was no more effective than a placebo in children with trichotillomania. Even with this discouraging study, we know that NAC has no known significant side effects and is therefore safe in children and may be worth trying. Inositol may also be a good option.

2. Although habit-reversal therapy has demonstrated some benefit for trichotillomania and excoriation disorder, finding trained therapists can be a challenge. For people who cannot find a trained therapist for in-person therapy, there are online versions of therapy for both disorders produced by the Trichotillomania Learning Center (www.trich.org).

Case

Susan is a woman in her mid-thirties who has a full-time job. She has no psychiatric history, but her skin picking and hair pulling have continued without a break since she was about 14 years old. The behaviors worsen during stress and have taken a toll on Susan's self-esteem over the years. She does not think she is nice looking, so she does not date, and she does not ask for promotions at work because she doesn't think she deserves them: "Someone who cannot control this behavior does not deserve control over more responsibilities at work."

Susan had never previously sought treatment because she just assumed these "bad habits" were a sign of her lack of willpower or emotional strength or were more generally a character flaw. After she saw a television program on trichotillomania, however, she asked her family doctor about the behavior. He prescribed an SSRI antidepressant, telling her that her behavior was likely just a manifestation of anxiety. The medication helped for about one month, with some reduction in pulling and picking, but thereafter everything returned to how it had been, with daily picking and pulling. When Susan came to our clinic, she had assumed she was untreatable. Her lack of response to the SSRI left her feeling demoralized and hopeless.

Education about trichotillomania and excoriation disorder were provided at the first visit. We told Susan that in fact she had never had any real treatments for her behaviors, so rather than being "untreatable," she was fresh to treatment. In addition, a physical examination of her picking was performed to see if any infections were present that would demand more detailed treatment. After that, we provided weekly habit-reversal therapy with some dialectical behavior therapy elements and started her on NAC. The pulling and picking were quite severe, and we thought Susan's disorder would improve faster by doing both treatments together.

Susan responded well to treatment, staying in therapy for eight months and continuing on NAC for a year. She has continued with good improvement but with some episodic bouts of picking or pulling, particularly when under extreme stress, although she has been able to control the severity of these episodes. She reports feeling more confidence in her ability to manage her hair-pulling and skin-picking episodes when they start, which has translated to more confidence in the workplace.

Key Points for Individuals with Hair Pulling or Skin Picking

1. These behaviors are not just bad habits, and people can improve with appropriate treatment.
2. Do not accept the diagnosis that these habits are the same as obsessive-compulsive disorder.
3. Do not accept the advice that you should just be able to stop on your own if you try harder.
4. Do not accept the observation that you are doing it for attention or that it is the same as self-injury.
5. Educate yourself about trichotillomania and excoriation disorder, because many physicians do not know anything about these behav-

iors, and you may have to educate them or ask them to educate themselves about your problem.

6. Explore the website www.trich.org for referrals, support groups, and other information.

7. Even if it might be embarrassing, you must let your health care provider know if you are swallowing hairs, because this could be a serious health problem.

8. Tell your physician about picking in areas that cannot be seen, so the doctor can examine you to assess whether the picking has been deep and is causing a serious health problem.

Key Points for Family Members

1. Family members should educate themselves about trichotillomania and skin-picking disorder. An excellent website is www.trich.org, which is full of information about these disorders.

2. Family members need to know that hair pulling and skin picking are not the same as self-injurious behaviors such as cutting.

3. These behaviors are not the result of bad parenting and are not a reflection of early abuse.

4. Family members may say "Just stop it," but this command does not help and may produce more shame. Instead, loved ones might try asking the person, "How can I help you control your behavior?"

5. Family members should encourage the person to get appropriate treatment for the behaviors.

10

Causes of Behavioral Addictions

I t is natural to wonder why some people develop behavioral addictions and other people do not. In answering the question, "What causes mental illnesses?" we are addressing this very human need to know, and we are finding ways to intervene and help people avoid developing these conditions in the first place.

Different tiers of understanding

There is no single cause of behavioral addictions. As we describe in the chapters on specific behavioral addictions, multiple factors *in combination* cause behavioral addictions. These factors can be categorized roughly as biological causes, genetic causes, and environmental causes. Neuroscience attempts to understand behavioral addictions from the perspective of neurobiology (brain circuits and functions); psychology focuses on models of mental functions and behaviors; and sociology (as applied to mental disorders) homes in on how the concept of mental disorders develops and is influenced by social norms and such dynamics as geopolitics and institutions.

Different aspects of these illnesses can be seen from various vantage points that are not mutually exclusive. It is helpful to think of an individual as having a biological hierarchy: at the root are *genetic factors*, which have massive influences on *brain structure and function*; the brain, in turn, is responsible for *cognitive processes* underlying our thoughts and actions; and these cognitive processes then lead to our *observable behavior*. Each of these levels (genes, brain structure and function, cognitive abilities, overt behavior) is influenced by its interactions with a host of environmental factors throughout a person's life. For example, the development of the fetus is influenced by maternal factors (nutrition, substance use, and stress); the development of a child is influenced by parenting styles, the home milieu, schooling, interactions with others (children and adults); and teenage development is influenced by additional factors such as substance use, diet, exercise, and work. Other environmental factors include society's ideas about what is "normal" and what constitutes a "mental disorder"; societal expectations for behavior; and sociocultural recognition of and attitudes toward mental illnesses.

Are behavioral addictions inherited?

It is very unlikely that any behavioral addiction is due to one specific genetic abnormality. *Heritability* is defined as the proportion of the occurrence of a disorder that is attributable to genetic differences between people. Most mental health conditions show some degree of heritability, but as far as we know, many genes are involved, each of which confers only a small degree of risk in itself.

Heritability of disorders can range from 0 percent (meaning that genes are completely unimportant) to 100 percent (meaning that genes account for virtually all risk). As described in earlier chapters, the gold standard type of study for assessing heritability of any condition is the examination of monozygotic twins (identical twins, who share all, or nearly all, important genetic information) compared to dizygotic twins (fraternal twins, who share roughly half of important genetic information). Published twin studies for behavioral addictions are few and do not exist at all for several of the disorders discussed in this book. Heritability for trichotillomania has been estimated at around 76 percent; for Internet addiction, 60 to 65 percent; for gambling disorder, 50 to 60 percent; and for excoriation (skin-picking) disorder, 40 percent. To our knowledge there are no published genetic heritability data for compulsive sexual behavior, food addiction, compulsive stealing (kleptomania), or compulsive buying. In all, then, for those behavioral addictions for which we have data, around 40 to 60 percent of the occurrence of these conditions can be attributed to genetic factors, a similar percentage attributable for substance addiction and many other mental health conditions. To an extent, the risk of developing a behavioral addiction is inherited, but environmental factors are roughly as important as genetic ones.

What does this genetic involvement mean in real terms for people with behavioral addictions and their families? Most important, and because heritability is only partial, one or both parents having a behavioral addiction makes it far from inevitable that their children will also develop a behavioral addiction. The bottom line is that offspring of people with behavioral addictions are at increased chance of also developing a behavioral addiction, but the vast majority will not, which is reassuring. Potential parents should not decide against having children just because they have experienced a behavioral addiction that they don't want to pass on. In fact, if parents have experienced a behavioral addiction and are familiar with symptoms and treatments, they can be helpful if similar symptoms do start to occur in their children. They will recognize the symptoms early and get early treatment, preferably before the behavior is thoroughly established.

Are genetic tests useful?

The risk of developing one or more behavioral addictions is likely to be affected by many genes, each of which confers only a small element of risk in itself. Genetic studies in mental health are notoriously inconsistent: vast sample sizes are needed to detect a specific gene's association with a mental illness, because the effect of that gene is likely to be very small. Some findings are likely to be *false positives*—in other words, they are statistical anomalies driven by chance findings, and are not a true genetic effect. Because of issues with genetic studies and the test results, there is no genetic test at this time that would be useful to predict an individual's chance of developing a behavioral addiction, to predict outcomes in advance, or to help choose the best types of treatment to use. The hope is that eventually it might be possible to develop algorithms based on genetic tests and other biological markers to guide treatment. But for now, we do not recommend genetic tests at the individual level in behavioral addictions.

Is male or female gender "causal"?

Gender does not cause the development of a behavioral addiction, but certain behavioral addictions are more common in one gender, or differ as a function of gender in terms of how the symptoms develop over time.

Hair-pulling and skin-picking disorders are six to eight times more common in women than in men. The reasons for this are unclear. Grooming, such as plucking eyebrows, is more common behavior in women and is not generally regarded as socially "acceptable" or "normal" in men. Because milder forms of grooming predominate in women, we would expect more women than men to engage in more extreme types of grooming too—assuming that the one can develop from the other, which is a reasonable supposition. Also, men may be more able than women to conceal hair loss and skin lesions, more likely to attribute them to other causes, or less likely to seek help from family members and professionals.

There are also some gender differences for these conditions based on the way they present clinically. Men with trichotillomania have been found to experience (on average) pulling from more body sites, later age of symptom onset, worse functional impairment, and greater chances of co-occurring problems with anxiety. For excoriation disorder, one study found that men rate themselves as less attractive than other men (more so than women do), and that women had higher levels of depression. Men with excoriation disorder also consume disproportionately more alcohol than women with the condition.

Other behavioral addictions are also more common in women than in men, but not so strongly as for trichotillomania and excoriation disorder. Kleptomania (compulsive stealing) is about twice as common in women, while compulsive buying disorder is around two to four times more common in women. The female predominance in kleptomania and compulsive buying disorder may result from cultural forces that have historically placed women in domestic spheres, where they do the shopping for the household, as well as the disproportionate number of advertisements for products and shopping targeted at women. Next to nothing is known about how gender affects the presentation of kleptomania and compulsive shopping—when it starts or how its symptoms progress. Food addiction may also be more common in women, perhaps because women may be more sensitive to the rewarding properties of food, especially sweet food such as chocolate. There is evidence that around the time of menstruation, women crave sweet food as a means of regulating hormone levels. Chocolate contains biologically active chemicals, including substances that act like caffeine (to increase arousal), and is also capable of calming or soothing. Food addiction is associated with similar overall functional impairments in men and in women, but comorbid depression is disproportionately more common in women with the condition.

Substance use disorders in general are more common in men than in woman, and certain forms of behavioral addiction are too: namely, gambling disorder (5 times more common in men), compulsive sexual behavior (2 times more common), and Internet addiction (2 times more common, although age and geographical location affect the ratio). For gambling disorder, men tend to develop the disorder earlier than women and prefer so-called strategic types of gambling, such as sports betting, betting on horse races, or playing cards, while women prefer so-called nonstrategic types of gambling, such as slot machines, lottery tickets, or bingo. Men are more driven by the rewarding nature of gambling, while women tend to gamble as a means of reducing depressive and distressing feelings, as well as to avert loneliness. Although women start gambling later than men, they show a more rapid progression of symptoms toward gambling disorder, a phenomenon referred to as telescoping. Gambling disorder in women is associated with higher levels of anxiety and depression, higher levels of substance use disorders, greater chances of seeking help, and worse long-term outcomes on average.

The higher rates of compulsive sexual disorder in men may reflect casual sexual behaviors being more common in men, with around 30 percent reporting that their previous sexual act with another person was "casual," compared with 14 percent of women. Men also have more sexual fantasies than women and become sexually aroused more easily. There are also differences in societal attitudes about sexual behavior: in men, having many sexual partners can be perceived as status enhancing by peers and society, while in women, having many sexual partners can be very stigmatizing. In women with compulsive sexual disorder, there is a stronger association with social phobia, substance use disorders, and personality disorders. It has been speculated that compulsive sexual acts reflect a way of regulating mood or anxiety, especially in women, serving to reduce a depressed mood or anxiety, at least in the short term. It is not known whether the particularly strong association between social phobia and compulsive sex disorder in women is explained by compulsive sexual behaviors regulating anxiety or by sex acts leading to increased anxiety in the long term.

Greater compulsive Internet use in men might reflect what the Internet is being used *for*: gaming and pornography use are particularly common behaviors in this condition, are especially rewarding types of behavior, and are more common in men regardless of whether they use the Internet for these behaviors. In adolescents with Internet addiction, aggression is more common in males than in females, perhaps reflecting different coping strategies, and there is a stronger genetic influence on the disorder in males.

In sum, gender is not *causal* in behavioral addictions, but it does influence what types of behavioral addiction an individual is more likely to suffer from, for various complex, interacting reasons, including perceived social norms and hormonal factors. Trichotillomania, skin-picking disorder, food addiction, kleptomania, and compulsive buying are more common in women. By contrast, gambling disorder, compulsive sexual behavior, and Internet addiction are more common in men. Gender has important clinical implications for behavioral addictions because it can influence age of onset, rapidity of progression, and likelihood of seeking treatment.

Parenting styles and behavioral addictions

Parents often worry, feel guilty, and believe they might be responsible when they find out that their child (whether teenager or adult) has developed a behavioral addiction. There is no convincing evidence that "bad parenting" is responsible for the development of these conditions, and framing questions about causality in these terms can be stigmatizing and unhelpful. The etiology, or causes, of these conditions are multiple, complex, and only partially understood. Instead of asking whether parents are "to blame," it is more helpful to think about whether family environmental factors could predispose or encourage a path toward or away from the development of behavioral addictions.

Studies have repeatedly demonstrated that adults with substance addiction report, on average, a greater history of having received certain parenting styles: in particular, styles characterized by lower perceived care but overcontrol. These retrospective reports suggest that particular parenting styles can predispose toward substance addictions. Might the same be true for behavioral addictions, since they share some similarities with substance addictions? Several studies have indeed reported that lower perceived parental care coupled with higher parental overprotectiveness were associated with gambling disorder in adults. Parenting styles characterized by rejection and a high degree of psychological control have also been strongly implicated in food addiction and other types of eating disorders. In adolescents with compulsive Internet use, higher levels of perceived parental overinvolvement, less emotional warmth, and more rejection were reported, compared with controls (those without Internet addiction). Little is known about possible links between perceived parenting styles and other behavioral addictions, namely kleptomania, compulsive shopping, trichotillomania, excoriation disorder, and compulsive sexual behavior.

On the basis of the above evidence, we recommend that parents with children who have developed a behavioral addiction carefully consider their approach to rearing children: we can all fall into habitual ways of interacting with others. When parents are worried that family dynamics might be contributing to behavioral addiction in children, it can be useful to seek treatment with family therapy, which involves working with different family members to explore and change dynamics without trying to place blame on individuals.

Does diet play a role?

There is no convincing evidence, so far, that the types of food we eat can cause, or prevent, the majority of behavioral addictions. However, food intake is of course directly relevant to understanding food addiction and—to a lesser extent—gambling disorder. In food addiction, there may be recurrent episodes in which an individual eats disproportionate amounts of food and experiences a loss of control. Craving for unhealthy food and the temporarily relieving effects of a food binge contribute to the persistence of the symptoms but also lead to obesity. Dietary interventions (weight-loss programs) are vital in treating food addiction associated with obesity, because treating only food addiction with psychotherapy is unlikely to lead to much weight loss.

Gambling disorder is associated with increased risk of obesity. This may be a consequence of the sedentary nature of some types of gambling, where players are seated for long periods playing bingo or at the casino. People with gambling disorder are also more likely to avoid regular exercise, to consume alcohol, and to watch television for more than twenty hours each week. Again, for these reasons it is important to intervene not just for the gambling disorder itself but also for the obesity, with targeted and evidence-based treatment interventions.

Beginning to understand the behaviorally addicted brain

The following introduction to how the brain usually operates helps explain how brain processes contribute to behavioral addictions. The human brain is a very complex organ: on average, an adult human brain contains more than 80 billion neurons, electrically excitable cells that process and transmit information. Each of these cells forms connections, or *synapses*, with other neurons, making for a total of 100 to 500 trillion (that is, 100 to 500 million million) synapses in the human brain of an average adult. With these trillions of connections, it shouldn't be surprising that the science of the mind (psychology, psychiatry, and neuroscience) has struggled to capture and explain the underlying processes in the brain that can account for our behaviors and thoughts! The brain is also far from a static organ; it was originally thought that the development of the brain's structure ended during childhood, but now it is recognized that the brain's structure does not resemble that of a "completed adult" until people reach their early to mid-twenties. Even then, the structure can still change over time, such as in response to environmental changes, hydration, nutritional status, aging, and disease. The brain can also change functionally: through rewiring and changes in the chemical modulation of circuits, the brain is an incredibly adaptive organ throughout life.

The brain can essentially be considered in terms of distinct interconnected structures, or regions, with relatively specialized functions. The *cortex* is the brain's outermost layer, shielded by the skull, and exists in humans and other mammals; it is divided into two hemispheres and is just 2 to 4 millimeters thick on average. Because the human cortex is folded, forming ridges and fissures, a relatively large surface area can fit into the available space. The cortex is responsible for higher-level functions, including complex motor movements, different types of memory, the ability to plan (executive planning), attention, emotional processing, flexible learning, and the ability to suppress or stop impulsive and compulsive acts (referred to as *inhibitory control*). In deeper parts of the brain are structures that are relatively ancient in evolutionary terms; these structures are involved in our more primitive drives (for example, obtainment of food, shelter, sex), and in the development of habits. The striatum includes the nucleus accumbens (also referred to as the *ventral striatum*), which is a core part of the brain's reward circuitry, and the putamen and caudate (*dorsal striatum*), which regulate our habits. As we undertake behaviors that are initially rewarding, these behaviors over time can become more habitual and automatic, less driven by reward; this change over time is thought to be accompanied by a shift in the neural regions controlling the given behavior from the ventral to the dorsal striatum.

What might go wrong in the addicted brain?

Because the neurobiology of substance addictions has been more comprehensively studied than the neurobiology of behavioral addictions, substance addiction is a useful starting point in looking at what brain circuitry is likely to be involved in behavioral addictions.

Research in humans and animals has demonstrated that consuming a drug with addictive potential activates the brain's reward system, especially the nucleus accumbens (reward center), leading to increases in dopamine signaling (dopamine being one of a handful of important neurochemicals in the brain responsible for controlling important high-level cognitive functions and behaviors). These effects on the brain's dopamine reward system account for the reinforcing potential of certain substances. Drugs that do not affect this reward system are not generally addictive.

In developing a substance addiction, individuals crave an increasing amount of a given addictive substance and start to neglect other areas of life, because the drug acts as a positive reinforcer and because not taking the drug can lead to withdrawal effects (such as shaking, sweating, anxiety, and fidgetiness). These psychological processes are referred to as *operant conditioning*. *Classical conditioning* also plays a role: environmental cues (such as the place where drugs were previously taken, the appearance or smell of the drug) become associated with the pleasurable aspects of drug seeking, which means that exposure to these cues for whatever reason can trigger irresistible cravings.

Over time, operant and classical conditioning take their toll on the increasingly addicted individual. Continued drug use leads to changes in the dopamine transmitter system, for example, reducing the availability of dopamine receptors in the reward center, which is believed to lead to the need to take increasingly large amounts of drugs to obtain the same reward. The reward center becomes increasingly preoccupied with drug-related stimuli: a sort of "hijacking" of the circuitry. Over time, there is a shift toward the drug use becoming habitual rather than driven by reward. Drug-addicted individuals in the later stages of their addiction tend to report feeling compelled to take drugs, not because they enjoy it, but simply because they cannot stop themselves. The brain regions involved shift from the reward center (ventral striatum) to the putamen-caudate structure (dorsal striatum).

Another neurobiological factor involved in drug addiction is cognitive impairment. People with substance addictions often show problems in various cognitive domains, particularly inhibitory control—the ability to suppress impulsive and compulsive acts. Some of these cognitive problems may be a consequence of the damaging effects of chronic substance use on the brain. It has recently been discovered, however, that unaffected first-degree relatives of people with substance addictions already show problems with impulse control (response inhibition): put differently, impaired inhibitory control probably represents a *vulnerability marker*, or predisposing factor, toward substance addiction, rather than being purely a consequence of it. This finding is of clinical relevance because these cognitive impairments could represent a new early treatment target, to help stem the chance of developing a substance addiction before it occurs in people at high risk.

The gambling brain

Of the behavioral addictions, neural circuits involved in gambling disorder have received the most study so far.

The act of gambling for a person with gambling disorder produces a sense of euphoria akin to that experienced by a substance addict consuming a drug. Does gambling activate the brain's reward center in a similar way to substances of abuse? The answer to this question is not completely clear. There is some evidence that dopamine activity in the brain increases during a gambling task, which relates both to subjective levels of excitement and to decision-making impairment on the task. There is also some evidence that dopamine activity in the brain correlates with gambling symptom severity and other measures of impulsivity in people with gambling disorder.

Abnormal activation in the nucleus accumbens (ventral striatum) has been identified in people with gambling disorder compared with healthy controls (those without gambling disorder or other mental illness). These findings were derived from functional neuroimages that measured brain activation as volunteers played computer tasks while lying in a brain scanner. For example, people with gambling disorder show reduced striatal responses during reward anticipation as well as in response to winning money. Another study found that gamblers show relatively increased brain sensitivity to money than to erotic stimuli, supporting the idea that—in gambling addiction—gambling-related stimuli hijack the brain's reward circuitry. Abnormal brain activation during gambling-related stimuli has been found not only in the reward center but also in the prefrontal cortices involved in inhibitory control (meaning the ability to stop oneself from engaging in a behavior).

On average, people with gambling disorder show some selective cognitive problems compared to those without the condition. Gambling disorder is associated with less advantageous decision-making abilities in general, while more severe forms of gambling disorder are associated with response-inhibition impairment and less flexible response on cognitive tasks. Decision-making impairments are found in people at risk of developing gambling disorder even before the symptoms become pathological, suggesting that this cognitive deficit may be a vulnerability or a risk factor; inhibitory and cognitive flexibility deficits, on the other hand, seem to occur only in those who have developed the disorder already.

The excessively grooming brain

Little research has been done on the neurobiological underpinnings of grooming disorders such as trichotillomania and excoriation (skin-picking) disorder. There are a handful of neuroimaging studies and some cognitive studies.

Using a functional neuroimaging task, people with trichotillomania showed dampened neural responses in the nucleus accumbens for reward anticipation, but relative overactivity for gain and loss outcomes, compared with controls (that is, people without trichotillomania), suggesting some parallels with substance addiction and gambling disorder. For trichotillomania, there is evidence for subtle changes in brain structure, including increased gray matter density of the dorsal striatum (caudate and putamen) and in the frontal cortex. White matter tracts, which connect these brain regions, also appear to be less organized than they should be in people with trichotillomania compared with controls. It is important to note that these are very subtle differences and may well relate to a genetic predisposition toward this disorder, rather than being a consequence of the habit. In support of this idea, at least in terms of the gray matter findings, excessive cortical thickness in the right frontal lobe and other regions has been identified both in people with trichotillomania and in their symptom-free first-degree relatives, compared with people who have no known family history of the condition, suggestive of a vulnerability marker.

In skin-picking disorder, one study found excess volume of the ventral striatum and reduced cortical thickness in the right frontal lobe compared with controls. In a separate study, skin-picking disorder was associated with less organized white matter tracts than found in people without the disorder, in regions extremely similar to those found to be abnormal in trichotillomania in an independent study.

Cognitive deficits have been reported in some but not all studies of people who have trichotillomania. Problems with inhibitory control have been found in people with trichotillomania and in their clinically asymptomatic first-degree relatives, suggesting a trait marker, as well as in people with skin-picking disorder.

The stealing brain

The neural correlates of compulsive shoplifting have barely been studied, in part due to lack of research funding and in part because people with this condition are understandably reluctant to admit to their behavior for fear of the potential legal consequences.

In the only brain imaging study so far, kleptomania was associated with reduced organization of white matter tracts in frontal brain regions compared with controls. What this means is not exactly clear, but it suggests that the connections between parts of the brain involved in controlling behavior or impulses are not particularly strong. This may explain why people with kleptomania seem to know that they should not engage in stealing but cannot seem to stop the behavior.

In terms of cognitive abilities, one study found that people who had stolen in the preceding year had decision-making impairments on a computerized test and some minor working memory impairments, especially on hard levels of a task; the other cognitive functions that were measured were normal.

The buying brain

Next to nothing is known about the neurobiology of compulsive buying or shopping. In a pilot study, individuals with compulsive buying showed impaired inhibitory control, decision making, and working memory compared with controls, suggesting some parallels with other behavioral addictions. Do these cognitive problems explain the excessive buying, are they due to excessive buying, or do they have nothing to do with the behavior? The question cannot be answered by available research at the present time. The findings do suggest that compulsive buying may be a symptom of the underlying inability to make good decisions and control one's impulses.

The sexual brain

There are few neuroimaging and cognitive studies of compulsive sexual behavior to date, probably for similar reasons as for kleptomania, but with the additional difficulty that researchers have yet to agree on an accepted definition for the condition.

Viewing erotic pictures activates the brain's reward circuitry, including the nucleus accumbens, and cortical regions such as the prefrontal lobe. Spending hours viewing pornography every week has been shown to correlate significantly with less gray matter volume in the right dorsal striatum, and with higher brain activation during viewing of sex-related cues in the dorsal striatum. In a brain-scanning study conducted in people with compulsive sexual behavior, enhanced responses to erotic videos were identified, compared with nonaddicted individuals, in the ventral striatum and anterior cingulate cortex, the latter of which is involved in action monitoring. Compulsive sexual behavior is related to the dopamine reward system, and dopamine medication used in Parkinson's disease has been linked with sexual behavior (and other impulsive behaviors, including gambling) in some people.

Whether cognitive problems exist in compulsive sex disorders is not yet clear, except for a reasonable body of evidence indicating that such individuals show attentional processing bias toward erotic stimuli.

The food-addicted brain

As with compulsive sexual behavior, there are few neuroimaging and cognitive studies in food addiction, in part because of problems defining and identifying this disorder. Most of the available research in this area has instead focused on the broader notion of obesity. Food addiction probably involves dysregulation not only of the brain reward system and cortical regions, but also of the more primitive *peripheral-hypothalamic* feedback system involved in satiety and calorie intake. This complexity differentiates food addiction from the other behavioral addictions. The peripheral-hypothalamic feedback system is quite difficult to assess in humans.

In a study that compared obese and lean individuals using functional brain imaging, people with obesity showed unusually strong activation of key brain regions (the striatum, frontal cortex, insula, and amygdala) in response to their favorite-food cues. Brain activation in obese people, but not in lean people, correlated significantly with a measure of insulin resistance.

In a separate study, obese people showed reduced dopamine receptor binding in the brain's reward center (striatum) compared with normal weight individuals, and this dopamine abnormality correlated with higher body mass index. Another study did not replicate this finding, however.

Cognitive deficits related to decision making and response inhibition (inhibitory control) have been found in obese people. It is not yet known whether these deficits are vulnerability (predisposing) factors, or whether they are a consequence of eating too much or having a diet that is not optimal for brain functioning. It was also found that obese people were more likely to gamble, and to lose more money to gambling, compared with normal weight people, supporting the idea that food addiction overlaps to some degree with other types of behavioral addiction.

The Internet-addicted brain

There is a growing literature on the neurobiology of Internet addiction, mostly from parts of Asia, where Internet addiction is more recognized. Internet gaming addiction has been associated with reduced gray matter density in the frontal cortex, along with reduced white matter integrity in nearby regions. There have been approximately ten functional brain imaging studies, which overall have found excessive brain activation in Internet addicts in the frontal lobe and other cortical regions, across a range of computer tasks, compared with people who are not addicted to Internet use.

Some cognitive deficits have been described in Internet addiction, for example, in relation to aspects of mental flexibility and inhibitory control, but findings are less consistent than for other behavioral addictions. This may be because "Internet addiction" is not one thing, but rather refers to a collection of conditions in which the Internet is merely a means to an addiction rather than the core pathology of addiction itself.

Conclusions

There's neither a single cause nor a simple cause of behavioral addictions. When thinking about causes of behavioral addictions, it is helpful to bear in mind several distinct but complementary vantage points, including genetics, neurobiology, psychology, and society. There are no genetic or neurobiological markers identified so far that can reliably identify a person with a behavioral addiction, nor any markers that can accurately predict long-term outcomes or direct treatments. The research findings help to formulate *models*, or understanding, of disease but are of limited benefit to the affected individual. It can be reassuring to know, however, that behavioral addictions have a neurobiological basis, even if we do not fully understand it yet.

What does seem clear is that behavioral addictions are associated with subtle changes or abnormalities in brain regions involved in reward processing (nucleus accumbens, ventral striatum), habit drive (putamen and caudate, dorsal striatum), emotional processing (insula), and top-down control (frontal cortex). The dopamine neurochemical transmitter system is involved across these conditions, but other neurochemicals may play a role too, including opioids and noradrenaline.

People who have behavioral addictions should not be blamed for their illnesses. Much like medical conditions such as diabetes, hypertension, or asthma, behavioral addictions have a physical component and are not simply a matter of a deliberate lack of self-control. The person literally cannot "just stop it."

11

How Can Family Members and Friends Help?

Timothy and Julia have been married for eight years, but Timothy found out about Julia's kleptomania only when Julia was arrested a few months ago, at which time she had to disclose a ten-year history of shoplifting to her husband. Timothy was distraught. He wanted to be supportive and help his wife with her distress, and yet he felt that he didn't know her. He thought he understood and shared values similar to his wife's, and then this happened. Timothy was confused, but he was also very angry—about the potential for unknowingly being involved in illegal behaviors, and the fact that she did not trust him enough to tell him sooner. The anger in turn made him feel guilty. He loved his wife, and yet now he felt intensely angry at her.

What could or should he do to help her? He had so many questions, but he did not want to burden her with them. Should he talk to a psychiatrist? Was he partly to blame for Julia's stealing? Was she shoplifting because he was a bad husband? Was she trying to tell him something by this behavior?

When Julia started therapy, her counselor asked Timothy to attend a session or two. He refused. He did not feel able to discuss their marriage, and he did not want to be a part of her life, at least not at the time. He wanted to divorce her. He couldn't trust her anymore. In the evenings she cried, and he stayed in the guest room. He could not look her in the eyes.

Taking into account each person's uniqueness and each relationship's complexities, in this chapter, we offer advice that may not address all problems that loved ones encounter but will cover many of them. Several of these strategies are admittedly difficult to use and can be frustrating to attempt. (But then, coping strategies of all kinds are often easier to understand in theory than to implement in practice.) One thing for loved ones to keep in mind is that these strategies may be easier to use effectively when the person is receiving treatment for the behavioral problem.

The loved one of a person who has a behavioral problem is seldom able to treat the problem; generally, treatment must be done with a professional who is trained in treating these addictions. What follows, then, are not treatment guidelines. Instead, they are strategies designed to improve the lives of the loved ones coping with the problems—although the strategies may help the person struggling with the addiction as well. Loved ones often feel powerless and helpless when people they care about are struggling and perhaps ruining their own lives. These strategies often help people cope with those feelings and reassure them that they can do something for the person with a behavioral addiction and not make the behavior worse.

Is my family member with this problem just selfish?

People who have a behavioral addiction may get so wrapped up in the behaviors that they ignore everyone and everything else. They forget important dates and appointments, they stop doing things with their children or partners, and they may not hold up their share of household duties and responsibilities. Even when they are physically present, individuals with these behavioral problems may be so preoccupied with the behaviors or consequences of the behaviors that they are not mentally present with loved ones. They might be sitting with the family at dinner, but in their minds they are strategizing about their next night of gambling, trying to head off embarrassing phone calls from sexual partners, or worrying about the potential legal consequences if anyone finds out what they did yesterday.

What causes this self-absorption into the addictive behavior? The self-centeredness could predate the behavior. Studies have found that people with kleptomania or addictions to gambling, buying, sex, or the Internet tend to have elevated rates of narcissism, which might explain the lack of concern for others. (A narcissistic person has an inflated sense of his own importance, has a higher than usual need for admiration, and lacks empathy for other people.) The behavioral problem creates a stress in the person's life, and that stress brings out the dysfunctional personality traits that loved ones never saw before. Alternatively, for some people, the problems associated with these behaviors become so great and so overwhelming that the individuals simply cannot attend to others or to daily activities because of their abject fear that their life is falling apart. In this latter case, once the behavior is well controlled, the individual can reconnect with the family. In the former case, the person may need some additional help with understanding and controlling the narcissistic traits.

Understanding what the person is going through

Family members often believe that the people who have behavioral addictions do not care about anyone but themselves, that they are selfish and unfeeling, and that they are not aware of how their behavior affects others. Although this may be true for some, in our experience, the people with these behaviors suffer greatly, and feel guilty, because of how their behavior affects their loved ones. Other than some truly narcissistic people, most individuals feel horrible guilt and shame about their behaviors. They feel remorse over letting loved ones down and over the possibility that they caused financial or legal problems for the people they care about.

Feelings of guilt and shame lead many individuals to isolate themselves from the family and not talk about the behavior or the consequences. "I can only say 'I'm sorry' so many times. My family wants explanations, and I don't have any. I would love some support, but I could never ask for any, because of what I have done to them."

A young woman with trichotillomania described her feelings in this way: "I feel horrible about my pulling, but I can't stop. The problem is that I also feel horrible about my mother's response to it. I know she wants me to stop and that I probably embarrass her. Her reaction just adds to my overall frustration with the behavior, and the stress makes me pull even more."

Getting caught up in the family member's addictive behavior

Enabling is the word often used to refer to the behavior of a loved one that perpetuates a problem or makes it worse. One way this happens is when a loved one makes accommodations for the person's addictive behavior. For example, Bob's girlfriend pays his rent each month because his gambling makes it impossible for him to do so. He tells her he will be homeless unless she helps, and so she thinks she is doing something positive for him even when her actions clearly allow him to continue his gambling behavior. Another way loved ones enable is to take the blame for the behavior. Martha, for example, has come to believe that if she were more attractive, her husband would not spend hours on the Internet looking at pornography. She blames herself for his behavior, and so, instead of setting limits with him, she allows it and is working to improve her appearance. The practical effects of these loved ones' behaviors is that the person with the addiction does not have to take responsibility for the behavior and may even be shielded from awareness of the harm it is causing.

Parents' perspectives

Coping with any of these behavioral problems may be particularly difficult for parents, because most parents feel responsible for their child's difficulties. Was this behavioral addiction their fault? If they had been better parents, would their child have this problem? What could they have done differently? A mother of a 20-year-old woman with skin-picking disorder described it this way: "I must have been a bad mother, otherwise she wouldn't do this. What can I do to correct the wrongs I did in the past?"

Because parents often blame themselves, they are often willing to enable their child even when they know that it may not be a good idea. The adult child may in fact foster the enabling. "I know my mother felt guilty about my gambling problem. She felt that I probably started doing it because she was always working. Now, when I need money for gambling, I just hint at the idea of her being a delinquent parent during my upbringing, and she is willing to give me money. I know it's not true, and I shouldn't do it, but I really want the money."

General approaches for family members and other loved ones

We begin with some general approaches for loved ones of a person with any behavioral addiction. In the next section, we address common decisions and problems that loved ones may encounter. Strategies for loved ones dealing with specific addictions are discussed later in the chapter.

Accept the diagnosis and take the behavior seriously

These behavioral addictions are serious illnesses and usually do not simply go away on their own. Family members must come to grips with the idea of their loved one having a behavioral addiction. Telling the person to simply stop doing the behavior will not work. Most people need to receive treatment for these behaviors. Family members should learn all they can about these disorders, preferably firsthand from a professional or through reliable resources (see the resources at the end of this book, for a place to start). We do not recommend getting information from blogs or from individual harangues on the Internet, many of which provide false information or false hope.

Talk openly about the behaviors

There is often significant embarrassment about these behaviors, especially about the criminal or moral aspects of many of them. Secrecy is not helpful and may in fact keep the behavior going.

Encourage mental health treatment

Mental health treatment in the form of therapy either with or without medication has demonstrated benefit for all of these behaviors. Many people seek treatment only because a concerned family member helps them to do so. Although people with behavioral addictions need to develop insight and get serious about therapy on their own, support from family members makes it more likely that they will pursue and follow up with treatment. Family members can remind the person about appointments, take him to appointments, encourage his improvement, and remind him about compliance with therapy at home or with medications.

Be firm with children

The impulse to protect children at any cost makes some parents incapable of being firm with them even in the face of addictive behaviors. "Tough love" may be the best approach. Older children with these behaviors need to understand that they are responsible for their actions and have to accept the consequences. They need to understand that the days of controlling parents or family are over, and they can only understand this if the family stands firm while providing appropriate support and love.

Be patient with the loved one and maintain hope

Although some people respond relatively quickly to treatment, many with behavioral addictions improve only after several months in treatment. Family members also need to recognize that slips back into behavior may occur, but they do not mean that the person is not getting better. Slips may be shorter and different. In these differences lie many of the features of early improvement—for example, the person was able to stop the slip before it got completely out of control, and she started back to treatment instead of feeling hopeless.

Do not blame yourself

Even though we believe that genetics, developmental issues, personal biology, and life events all may contribute to the development of a behavioral addiction, we do not know what exactly causes these behavioral problems. Even so, these behaviors do not seem to be a result of something the family did wrong. They are far too complex for a simple answer like that. Looking back on the past and asking what the family could have done differently is probably a waste of time and energy. Although relatives and friends need to think about how their current behaviors might influence the person, they should also recognize that the other person's behaviors are largely beyond their control. The family can, however, ask what they can do now to help the person overcome his problems.

Common problems encountered by loved ones of people with behavioral problems

Participation in the behavioral problems

Behavioral addictions can be difficult for families to cope with because the problem is really the degree to which the person engages in the behavior (except kleptomania, which is illegal at any level). Thus, many family members are confused about whether they should continue to engage in particular types of behavior themselves, now that a loved one has a problem with them. Many families enjoy going to the casino, going shopping, and playing games on the Internet. Some couples look at pornography together, and many families have various eating rituals, such as popcorn at night while watching television. When a family recognizes that someone has a problem with one of these behaviors, they have to negotiate whether others in the family can still do the behaviors and be clear about whether they are triggering behavior in the loved one.

Family members need to be able to have their own lives and not be held hostage by the loved one's problems, and this may mean continuing to shop, eating when they feel like it, and using the Internet. The family should, however, consider how to engage in these behaviors at times and in places where the loved one will not be triggered into the behavior as well. This may mean using the Internet in a private room and not asking the loved one to go shopping or gambling.

The loved one suffering from a behavioral addiction may ask family members not to engage in the behavior any longer. "Can you please respect my wishes? I have a problem with gambling, so I would like all of us to stay out of the casino." Family members should let the person know that they understand he is in pain, that he is struggling with this addiction, but that his pain and addiction do not mean that others need to change their lives. There is a fine line between flaunting one's behavior in the face of the addicted person to make him suffer versus doing things privately. Individuals with these behavioral addictions need to learn how to manage their behavior living in a world where many people engage in these same behaviors responsibly. It is not realistic for them to try to get everyone they know to give up things; doing so will often prompt anger, not support, from family members.

Denial of their problems

This is one of the aspects of behavioral addictions that is the most frustrating for family members. "Bill keeps telling me he is fine, that he was just in an odd phase of his life. He denies being a gambling addict and is constantly hounding me for money. I keep telling him that his counselor told us not to give him any money, and he gets angry and says his counselor doesn't know anything." Most family members refrain from having these conversations because they realize that no matter what they say, the debate continues.

We recommend that if family members engage these comments, they do so with a small "reality check." It can be useful to gently remind the person how their behavior dominated the person's life and what problems it caused, particularly when the person is receiving cognitive behavioral therapy, because the therapy helps highlight the person's distortions about their behavior. Sometimes, however, family members are understandably frustrated and have an angry response: "You're a gambling addict. You have ruined our family with your gambling, and your children resent you because of it." These harsh and unkind words may do more

harm than good. In this example, the gambler may feel that if the relationships are truly ruined anyway, then he may as well gamble. Try to use
constructive, supportive words; avoid referring to the individual as an
"addict."

Manipulation and lies

Many people with these behavioral addictions will manipulate family
members to get what they want and lie about the extent of the behavior
and the consequences. The person with kleptomania may lie to family
members that the therapy is helping and that she can go to the store alone
because her therapist told her to do so. Individuals with skin picking may
tell family they have stopped the behavior but in fact are just hiding the
areas of their body where they are picking. Family members want to believe that the person is better or that the crisis has passed, and so they
often believe these mistruths. A classic example is someone with a gambling problem who asks family for money, telling them that he has to
pay the rent immediately—and then gambles it all away.

The issue of dishonesty in people with behavioral addictions is complex. Oftentimes the person does not want to lie or manipulate loved ones
but does so anyway. She might tell family members, "It's the illness. I can't
help it." This is only partially true. Many people with behavioral addictions do not lie or manipulate. Why do some people lie? One explanation
could be the severity of the illness—the more severe the urges and the
consequences, the more likely someone is to lie and manipulate. Another
explanation could be the character of the person with the behavioral
addiction. Manipulative people can get mental health problems, and so the
lying and manipulation may not be restricted to that behavior and may
suggest other problems under the surface, which should be brought to
light in treatment.

Family members may want to meet with the therapist who is treating
the person with a behavioral addiction, to discuss the lies and manipu-
lations and to understand what is going on in therapy. Many people with
behavioral addictions lie to the family, telling them that their therapist
suggested x, y, or z, when in fact the therapist suggested nothing of the

sort. The problem is that without signed releases to talk with family, the therapist cannot explain things to them. Family members and the therapist are both being manipulated.

Loved ones may want to talk to the person about how continuing to lie and manipulate makes it difficult to rebuild trust. This could provide an incentive not only for honesty but also to continue to control behaviors. The problem arises when family members make statements suggesting that one more betrayal or lie is the final one. "I told my husband that if I ever caught him online with pornography again, I was going to leave him." This is not an uncommon feeling, particularly in the case of sexual compulsivity, but it does generate its own problems. If this is the "line in the sand" by the loved one, what does the sexually compulsive person do if he or she has looked at pornography again? Being honest means losing your partner, but being deceptive and lying means perpetuating the old behaviors. This is why we recommend that family and other loved ones avoid establishing rigid rules that make the person feel he is not able to make any mistakes. As the behavioral addiction responds to treatment, higher goals can be set, but all-or-nothing approaches are usually counterproductive. This does not mean that a loved one cannot decide to leave the addicted person because of his or her problem behavior; the decision to leave should be made based on multiple variables, however, and should not be based on one rule that is established and then broken.

Problems with overall functioning

Many people with behavioral addictions have difficulty functioning, and this difficulty often affects family members, especially parents of adolescents with these problems. The family member is often in the position of urging the adolescent to go to school, be on time for a job, or even get out of the house for any period. An adolescent with Internet addiction who is trying to give up Internet use may become despondent and sit in bed all day, unable to find things to excite or motivate. Often no friends are available because the person has severed those relationships as she pursued the addictive Internet use. People with trichotillomania or skin-picking disorder often avoid friends and work or school events because of embarrassment.

In our experience, family members are often quite willing to help with functioning, yet providing support may be a strain on their own resources, such as time and emotional strength. Family members may have to ask themselves if helping is really in the best interest of the person. For example, when it comes to young adult children, how long should the child stay with the parents and be financially dependent on them?

Family members need to encourage better functioning and at the same time recognize the person's limitations due to struggles with the behavior. There are no simple solutions to this problem. Family members may need to work with a therapist to see which approach is best for them. The goal for adults should be independent functioning and self-support. The path to get there and the pace of getting there need to be tailored for the individual and the family.

In general, idleness is not healthy for someone with these behaviors, as these behaviors often fill the space when there is nothing else to do. Therefore loved ones should encourage the person to keep busy. Family members might consider creating lists of chores at home or job ideas. These projects could be done in a step-wise progression, perhaps starting with chores at home, moving to a part-time job, and then something full time. It may take longer to improve functioning than to stop the behavior. Many people who stop a behavior take months to improve their functioning. Family members should be supportive and provide positive feedback along the way while remaining vigilant to lapses back into their loved ones' old behaviors.

Reluctance to get or stay in treatment

People with behavioral addictions report enormous amounts of ambivalence about their behaviors. They don't want to have problems from the behaviors, and yet they do not want to stop them either. Many people have said things remarkably similar over the years about their behaviors: "I don't want to stop gambling. I just want to stop losing." "I don't dislike stealing. I hate getting caught." "The food binges are not the problem. The weight gain is the problem." "I like picking my skin. I just don't like the way it looks afterward." These comments reflect the internal push and pull of these behaviors, people knowing they should stop but not wanting to stop.

Many people stop therapy or do not even go to therapy in the first place because of ambivalence and inner conflict. Family members are often surprised by these responses. They see nothing positive about the behaviors, so they are baffled by what they perceive as a lack of desire to correct the problem. As health care providers, we have often noted that people who call for treatment often do so after a big event, such as an arrest, a fight with a spouse, or a difficult financial situation. If they wait a few days before getting an appointment, we often never see them in our clinic. The intense turbulence passes, and then the motivation to stop a behavior dwindles.

Family members need to stress that treatment is not only about stopping a behavior but also about diminishing emotional pain, family strife, and feeling out of control. Effective treatment is worth trying. Family members may also remind the person that treatment is not for the rest of her life. The person should be told that having control over one's life is exciting and that the behavior has been the one in control up to now. Our patients commonly describe treatment as "freeing," as the burdens being lifted—the burden of being out of control, of acting secretively, and of doing things while weighed down with a sense of desperation. Being in control of their own life, instead of the excitement of the behavior, can be the new goal for people in treatment for behavioral addictions.

Feeling isolated

Family members dealing with a loved one who has a behavioral addiction may feel that they are the only ones who have a family problem such as this. They may feel stigma associated with having a person with a mental health problem in the family, and the additional stigma, for many of these behaviors, of having a family member with criminal problems. Shame often keeps loved ones from confiding in their friends, and not being able to talk things over with their friends may intensify feelings of isolation and loneliness.

Loved ones need to remind themselves that these behaviors are in fact common. Millions of family members are trying to make sense of these behaviors and cope with them. We encourage family members to confide their feelings in someone they trust. Most people are neither judgmental about nor shocked by these revelations and often know of someone else who has these behaviors. When a loved one struggles with compulsive sexual behavior or gambling problems, there are support groups for family members. Gam-Anon and S-Anon are two such groups, both of which have sections around the world. These are programs of recovery for those who have been affected by someone else's sexual or gambling behaviors. There are support groups for family dealing with the other behaviors as well, though they are not as widely available. Check your community's resources.

Suicidal thoughts

Our research and clinical experience, and that of others, tells us that suicidal thoughts are very common and recurrent in people with behavioral addictions. All of these behaviors are associated with greater levels of suicidal thoughts and attempts compared with the general population. A loved one's comments about suicide are very disturbing for family members, who naturally wonder what they should do about them.

If the person is not in treatment for her behavior, family members should encourage her to seek treatment, particularly if the person is voicing suicidal thoughts. Such comments should be regarded as a serious warning sign for families, who should seek help for their loved ones immediately. Family members may think that the person is just "blowing off steam" or "trying to get sympathy," and they may not take the threat seriously or may simply hope that it gets better on its own. This could be a huge mistake. The person's situation may become worse if she does not get effective treatment, and she may make a suicide attempt. Family members must help the person seek treatment.

Even during or after treatment, family members should be aware of a continued risk of suicidal thoughts and behaviors. We have seen several instances of a patient attempting suicide even after "successful" therapy. The impulse to take one's own life can be prompted by continued financial burdens or legal problems resulting from the behavioral addiction, because the person believes that his family would be better off without him: "My gambling is under control, but now I realize the extent of the financial burden I've placed on my family, and I have my pending court case because I embezzled money from my former employer to fund my gambling. I feel so ashamed and devastated. I put on a brave face for my wife, but I really think that she would be better off if I wasn't around." Importantly, "wasn't around" doesn't necessarily mean "divorce" or "separation." One cannot take such comments lightly; the person may in fact be referring to killing himself. Family members must be aware that suicidality can arise at any time and must encourage open dialogue with their loved one about such thoughts.

Behavior-specific suggestions for family and other loved ones

Moving now from advice for loved ones coping with issues involved in all behavioral addictions, we turn to specific behaviors. The unique aspects of these behaviors mean that the family issues differ somewhat as well.

Gambling

Among behavioral addictions, gambling has some unique issues for family members. The primary problem for families of gamblers is financial. Financial issues can take many forms, from credit card debt to bankruptcy and even to the loss of one's home. Depending on who in the family manages the money, family members may not be at all aware of the financial devastation until it is at a peak. For this reason, financial issues in a gambler's family may not be dealt with until everyone is in a crisis—and it is in a crisis that many people make poor decisions. Even so, as soon as a family is aware of a gambling problem, finances need to be examined, and a forward-looking financial plan should be put in place. A financial plan might look like this:

- The gambler gives up credit cards and ATM cards.
- The gambler's wages are put into someone else's account, and the gambler is given a weekly allowance.
- Bills are prioritized and paid in order of urgency and importance.
- The gambler is educated about the idea that this plan will be in place only until he can control his behavior; it is not permanent, and it does not suggest that he is incompetent.
- Family members with joint accounts need to separate their finances in case the gambler relapses.
- If the finances are complex, if there has been extensive damage from gambling, or if legal issues come up related to the finances, a financial accountant should be consulted.

The financial issues of gambling sometimes create two other problematic areas of concern: legal and interpersonal. Someone with gambling problems may have a range of legal issues that have arisen from the gambling or from the financial side of gambling. Gamblers often embezzle funds from work, for example, telling themselves that they are simply borrowing until they win big, when they will pay it back. If family members are discussing this topic with the gambler, they should ask about all financial and legal issues—but in a nonjudgmental way. The gambler may not respond if he feels he is being misunderstood. When any legal issue seems to be part of the gambling problem, family members should encourage the gambler to contact a lawyer, and they should consider getting their own lawyer, independent of their loved one's attorney. The reason for this is that the legal issues of the gambler may put certain family members in their own legal trouble, and a lawyer may have conflicts if representing both the gambler and the family member.

Many families have interpersonal issues because someone in the family has a gambling problem. In particular, domestic abuse is more common in these relationships than in the general population. These problems may be due to the finances and the secrecy and lying associated with gambling. Family members need to know that when domestic abuse occurs, it does not simply get better on its own; the partner suffering abuse needs to get out of the home. To think that she can fix the abusive gambler is wrong. Safety should be the primary focus. Some partners tell themselves, "He only gets upset when we discuss money, so I will take care of the bills, and we'll be fine." This not only is unlikely to be true, but may also be counter-therapeutic, because the gambler needs to confront the financial consequences of his behavior.

As mentioned above, when a loved one struggles with gambling problems, Gam-Anon may be a useful support group for family members. Gam-Anon is a program of recovery for those who have been affected by someone else's gambling behaviors. Its members and meetings help remind family members that they are not alone in having a loved one with a gambling problem.

Stealing

This behavioral addiction is somewhat distinctive among most psychiatric disorders discussed in this book, because a person who acts on the addiction to steal is breaking the law. Thus, legal issues are an integral part of kleptomania. Even if someone has not been arrested, there is always the threat of arrest, and family members need to know how to deal with these consequences.

Our research has long shown that most people with kleptomania never willingly tell anyone about the behavior, even when it has gone on for years. This is why many family members find out about the behavior when there are legal issues—because legal issues are the impetus for many people to tell the family. This then becomes a double whammy for family members: they have to cope with a loved one being out of control with shoplifting as well as the immediate crisis of a legal problem. It is therefore common for family members to feel intense anger instead of compassion toward the shoplifter.

The first step for the family of a kleptomaniac is to get as much education about kleptomania as possible, especially before doing something out of anger. The person with kleptomania often needs legal counsel, and so do many family members. Loved ones of a kleptomaniac may own several stolen items and not be aware of it. One husband many years ago asked his wife in front of us, "How much in the house is stolen?" She answered "Nothing." When he left the room, she admitted that furniture, kitchen utensils, and bathroom items were all stolen. Even after admitting her behavior to her husband, she couldn't bring herself to list the items she had stolen because she felt so much embarrassment in front of him.

Family members should never lie to police about theft committed by a loved one. They often believe this helps the person, especially parents of adolescents with kleptomania. Not only does lying implicate the family member in the illegal behavior, it is also counter-therapeutic. The person with kleptomania needs to take responsibility for her behavior. This does not mean that family needs to call police and report the loved one, but lying to the police is inappropriate. If family members recognize items in the house that were stolen, we suggest that they encourage the loved one who stole them to return them. If they were stolen years earlier, we suggest that family members encourage the person to donate the items to charity. The therapeutic goal for the person is to recognize that the items are a reflection of her illness. By getting rid of them, the person is giving herself a message: possessions should not have more value than integrity.

Parents often ask whether they should call the police when a child refuses to return a stolen item. There is no easy answer to this question. It depends on how often the stealing has been occurring, what is stolen, and how amenable the child is to treatment. With appropriate treatment, we expect children to return stolen items eventually. If the child does not follow treatment, continues to steal, and expects family silence to protect her, however, then calling the police would be appropriate and possibly therapeutic as well.

Family members may be a valuable element in the treatment of kleptomania. One aspect of the treatment is to have the person avoid going to stores unless necessary, and when the person must go to the store, she should go with someone else. Family members can be helpful by accompanying the kleptomaniac to stores. This should not be done as a means of spying on the person but simply to accompany her and let her know that if she has urges to steal, she should leave the store, and the family member will finish the shopping.

Sex

Compulsive sexual behavior (CSB) also generates unique family issues. Unlike the other behavioral addictions, CSB can significantly tear apart couples through the betrayal and lies, particularly when the behavior takes the form of infidelity. Partners often ask whether they should stay in or leave the relationship. We cannot answer this for them. Trust can be regained for some partners but not for others. It is important for partners to know that if they cannot trust the person any longer, that is not reflective of their shortcomings. Everyone feels things differently, and some people cannot overcome the betrayal of sexual infidelity. Partners often need their own therapists to process this revelation of sexual behavior.

One other issue that needs to be addressed by partners is their own health. When CSB involves relationships with others, there is a risk for transmission of disease, including HIV. Partners need to recognize this possibility and be tested for sexually transmitted infections. Seeing a physician for this purpose is often embarrassing for the partner. If the person is too embarrassed to go to her primary doctor, she can go to a free clinic and be tested anonymously.

Partners often blame themselves for the person's CSB, and this self-blame may lead them to excuse the behavior: "I cannot fault my husband. If I were slimmer, more attractive, or sexually adventurous, he would not have cheated on me." Although sexual "fit" is important in relationships, the behaviors of a person who has CSB are independent of that person's partner. This is an illness. It is not about the partner but about the person who is engaging in the sexual behavior and that person's problems with intimacy, self-esteem, and identity. This should not be about blame, but it should also not lead to excusing behaviors that are disrespectful to the partner and the relationship. Partners need to educate themselves about CSB, recognize what role they may play in helping the person get better, and not excuse behaviors that are hurtful to them.

As mentioned above, when a loved one struggles with sexual problems, S-Anon may be a useful support group for family members.
The members and meetings of a group such as S-Anon often remind
family members that they are not alone in having a loved one with a
sexual problem, and sharing with others may relieve some of the isolation and stigma the family member feels.

Internet

Internet addiction does not usually involve illegal behaviors, but the level
of dysfunction can be pronounced. The government of China has
attempted to get this behavior recognized as a public health emergency,
largely because of multiple deaths due to the behavior in China. These
deaths were apparently the result of dehydration and cardiac problems
in people who spent continuous hours on the Internet without drinking
or eating. We often see young adults failing in their college or university
courses, or even dropping out completely, because of their Internet use.
Family members are often conflicted, and they are unsure how to help
given that most of us need to use the Internet daily. How much is too
much time on the Internet? With it being so easy to access the Internet
(for example, via phones), how can family members help the person control his behavior?

Family members need to take the behavior seriously and not feel that
it is silly or insignificant because it involves the Internet. If they take it
seriously, they can often work effectively with the person's therapist to
help monitor the time allotted to the Internet while at home. This includes time on mobile devices with Internet capabilities such as smartphones and tablets. It may be necessary to insist that the person only use
the Internet while in the family room or when around others so that the
time and focus remain on essential uses, such as for school or work.
Family members can also engage the person in other activities that do
not rely on the Internet. In these ways, loved ones can feel helpful and in
fact help the person with this behavioral problem.

Excessive Internet use may not be about the Internet for everyone. It
may reflect a problem with gambling, sex, or shopping, and the Internet

is just the vehicle by which the person does these other behaviors. Family members therefore may discover that what they believed to be an Internet problem is in fact a different behavioral issue.

Food

Food addiction presents the family with problems involving a person's overall physical health. People with food addiction may become overweight or obese because of their secretive eating patterns and the types of food they eat. Family members should be aware of the health concerns and encourage the person to get regular health checkups and blood work if diabetes or high cholesterol is suspected. Many people avoid going to doctors; family members can make the process less frightening by offering to take the person to appointments.

Loved ones of a person with food addiction often worry that they contribute to the problem by having unhealthy food options at home. Although the overeating itself is not due to food item availability, what the person addictively eats is somewhat determined by what is readily available. Family members can therefore take this opportunity to discuss with the person how they can all, as a family, work toward healthier eating habits. When used with individual therapy, the family's commitment to healthier eating can be beneficial for the person who addictively eats.

Buying

Two problems arise with compulsive buying that are important for the family to educate themselves about and have some plan for addressing. The first problem, as in the case of gambling, is the financial consequences of the behavior. Compulsive shoppers often have significant amounts of credit card debt. These financial issues can obviously affect the credit rating of a spouse or partner as well, if accounts are jointly held. Therefore, family members should monitor their credit ratings, credit cards, and bank accounts. In addition, they should take away all credit and ATM cards from the compulsive shopper, if they agree. And they should block sites on the Internet where the person has shopped in the past.

Compulsive shopping is often blithely criticized as a silly, insignificant problem, particularly in light of bumper stickers and movies trivializing the "shopaholic." Compulsive buyers struggle with controlling the behavior and often feel significant shame about the financial consequences of the behavior. One woman we treated pawned her wedding ring to get cash to buy more things. She was devastated by her own behavior, and yet she couldn't control it.

The other issue for family members is that compulsive shoppers often have a problem with hoarding the items they buy. Should the family simply throw out all the items? Although many people often feel this will be helpful, we know that when the items are discarded, most hoarders replace the items over time. In addition, when the items are discarded without the supportive help of a therapist, many people with hoarding will exhibit significant emotional distress. This reaction may be more than the family can cope with. The person should be in therapy, and the discarding of hoarded items should be performed as part of the therapy. The adult children of older adults may find out about the compulsive buying problem when public health officials inform them about the hoarding problem. This involvement of officials is often embarrassing for family members, but they can use the incident as leverage to get the compulsive buyer to agree to treatment.

Hair pulling and skin picking

These behaviors are often very difficult for family members because they see their loved ones as destroying or harming themselves with the behavior. "She is so beautiful! Why does she do this?" A couple of reminders are important for family members. Many times, the hair pulling or skin picking is more bothersome to the family than to the person doing it. It is important to talk with the loved one and see how much if any distress she has about the behavior. Family members should not assume their distress equals the distress of their loved one.

Many family members often force the person into treatment when the person is not interested in stopping and is not really bothered by the behavior. This does not help anyone and may cause a substantial rift in family relationships. Instead, in cases of children old enough to make their own decisions, the family should discuss the behavior calmly with the person and see what she wants to do about it.

Another issue for family members is that they often confuse hair pulling and skin picking with self-mutilation or other self-injurious behaviors. They read about these other behaviors online, and the information they find there is often jarring to the family because it may suggest that the behavior is related in some way to early life sexual trauma, chronic personality disorders, or a range of dysfunctional behaviors such as violence and substance abuse. Family members need to know that hair pulling and skin picking are not the same as self-injury. Research over the years has consistently found that hair pulling and skin picking have little in common with self-injury. Family members often feel better when they learn that trichotillomania and excoriation are considered to be more like nail biting than self-mutilation.

Summary of recommendations for family members and other loved ones

Here we offer a few take-home points about the behavioral addictions discussed in this book.

These are serious behavioral problems. They are not trivial problems for people. These behaviors result in significant dysfunction and even suicide. Family members need to get as much education about them as possible.

Family members cannot treat them. Family members cannot treat the behavioral problem, which can be frustrating. They can, however, work with the therapist to promote healthier behaviors in their loved one.

Behavioral addictions often become family illnesses. These behaviors can lead to legal, financial, and trust issues within the family. Family members may need their own therapists, lawyers, and accountants. Loved ones of the person with an addiction need to think about their own well-being.

There is no one-size-fits-all family approach to behavioral addictions. Family members may hear that they should or should not do certain things to help their loved one. Even in this book, we have made suggestions based on our clinical experience, our research, and the medical literature. Our suggestions are based on the best knowledge available at this time. But truly, one size does not fit all; your family and your loved one are unique, and a custom approach to *your* problem is what is needed.

Most families in this situation do not know which course to follow. They are scared, frustrated, and angry. Family members should work with the loved one's therapist in helping their loved one recover. They also ought to take steps to improve their own well-being, including working with their own therapist or counselor who can help them in their specific situation.

RESOURCES

These resources provide a starting place for people with behavioral disorders and their families who are seeking information, counseling, and medical services. The list is not exhaustive, and inclusion in this list is not necessarily an endorsement of the treatment approaches used by the providers listed.

TREATMENT CENTERS
CENTERS THAT TREAT A RANGE OF BEHAVIORAL ADDICTIONS

University of Chicago: Addictive, Compulsive, and Impulsive Disorders Clinic
https://acid.uchicago.edu/page/clinical-treatment
(773) 834-3778
Chicago, Illinois (USA)

Stanford Obsessive-Compulsive and Related Disorders Clinic
http://ocd.stanford.edu
(650) 498-9111
Palo Alto, California (USA)

UCLA Impulse Control Disorders Clinic
www.semel.ucla.edu/clinic/impulse-control
(310) 825-9989
Los Angeles, California (USA)

Lindner Center of Hope
http://lindnercenterofhope.org/patients-families/treatments-programs/outpatient
(513) 536-HOPE (4673)
Mason, Ohio (USA)

Outpatient Clinic for Gambling and Other Impulse Control Disorders
Institute and Department of Psychiatry
University of São Paulo School of Medicine
Dr. Ovídio Pires de Campos
São Paulo (Brazil)

CENTERS THAT TREAT TRICHOTILLOMANIA AND EXCORIATION DISORDER
Informational Resources

Trichotillomania Learning Center
www.trich.org (a great resource, including a search tool for finding support groups and
treatment providers in different geographical areas)
(831) 457-1004

Outpatient Treatment
Massachusetts General Hospital: Trichotillomania Clinic and Research Unit
www.massgeneral.org/psychiatry/services/tricho_home.aspx
(617) 726-6766
Boston, Massachusetts (USA)

Western Suffolk Psychological Services
www.wsps.info
Huntington, New York (USA)

The Behavior Therapy Center of Greater Washington
www.BehaviorTherapyCenter.com
(301) 593-4040
Silver Spring, Maryland (USA)

Residential (Inpatient) Treatment
Rogers Memorial Hospital
https://rogershospital.org/residential-center/obsessive-compulsive-disorder-center
(800) 767-4411
Locations in Wisconsin and Florida (USA)

Outpatient Treatment: Children
Child and Adolescent OCD, Tic, Trich and Anxiety Group (The COTTAGe)
University of Pennsylvania
www.med.upenn.edu/cottage
(215) 746-1230
Philadelphia, Pennsylvania (USA)

UCLA Childhood OCD, Anxiety and Tic Disorders Program
www.semel.ucla.edu/caap
(310) 825-0122
Los Angeles, California (USA)

Online Treatment

www.stoppulling.com
www.stoppicking.com

CENTERS THAT TREAT GAMBLING DISORDER
United States

Columbia Gambling Disorders Clinic at the New York State Psychiatric Institute
www.columbiagamblingdisordersclinic.org
(646) 774-8096
New York, New York

Canada

Addictive Behaviours Laboratory
University of Calgary
www.addiction.ucalgary.ca
(403) 220-3118

Centre for Addiction and Mental Health
University of Toronto
Problem Gambling Treatment Services
www.camh.ca/en/hospital/care_program_and_services/addiction_programs/Pages
/guide_problem_gambling_srv.aspx
(416) 599-1322

Australia

University of Sydney Gambling Treatment Clinic
www.psych.usyd.edu.au/gambling_treatment_clinic/about_us/index.shtml
1-800-482-482

South Africa

Alexandra Hospital
University of Cape Town
www.health.uct.ac.za/fhs/departments/psychiatry/clinical/alexandra
021-503-5000

United Kingdom

National Program Gambling Clinic (NHS)
www.cnwl.nhs.uk/cnwl-national-problem-gambling-clinic
020-7381-7722

Denmark

Research Clinic on Gambling Disorders
Aarhus University Hospital
www.en.auh.dk/departments/head-neuro+centre/research+clinic+on+gambling
+disorders
45-7845-0000

Sweden

Stockholm Centre for Dependency Disorders
www.beroendecentrum.se/om-beroendecentrum/about-the-stockholm-centre—for
-dependency-disorders
08-123-400-00

South Korea

Korea Center on Gambling Problems
www.kcgp.or.kr/eng/center/Greeting.aspx
02-740-9000

CENTERS THAT TREAT COMPULSIVE SEXUAL BEHAVIOR

Program in Human Sexuality
University of Minnesota
www.sexualhealth.umn.edu
(612) 625-1500
Minneapolis, Minnesota (USA)

Pine Grove Behavioral Health and Addiction Services
www.pinegrovetreatment.com/index.php
(888) 574-HOPE (4673)
Hattiesburg, Mississippi (USA)

CENTERS THAT TREAT KLEPTOMANIA

Pathways Institute
www.pathwaysinstitute.net

(415) 267-6916
San Francisco, California (USA)

CENTERS THAT TREAT INTERNET ADDICTION

The Center for Internet Addiction
Bradford Regional Medical Center
http://netaddiction.com or www.brmc.com/programs-services/internet-addiction
-bradford-pa.php
(814) 368-4143
Bradford, Pennsylvania (USA)

reSTART
www.netaddictionrecovery.com
(800) 682-6934
Fall City, Washington (USA)

CENTERS THAT TREAT FOOD ADDICTION

Program for Obesity, Weight and Eating Research (POWER) at Yale
http://psychiatry.yale.edu/research/programs/clinical_people/power.aspx
(203) 737-5537
New Haven, Connecticut (USA)

READING RESOURCES
UNDERSTANDING BEHAVIORAL ADDICTION

Grant JE, Kim SW. *Stop Me Because I Can't Stop Myself: Taking Control of Impulsive Behavior.* McGraw-Hill, 2004.

GAMBLING

Blaszczynski A. *Overcoming Compulsive Gambling.* Robinson, 2010.
Petry N. *Pathological Gambling: Etiology, Comorbidity, and Treatment.* American Psychological Association, 2012.

STEALING

Abelson ES. *When Ladies Go A-Thieving: Middle-Class Shoplifters in the Victorian Department Store.* Oxford University Press, 1989.
Goldman MJ. *Kleptomania: The Compulsion to Steal—What Can Be Done?* New Horizon Press, 1997.

SEX

Carnes P. *Out of the Shadows: Understanding Sexual Addiction.* 3rd ed. Hazelden, 2001.
Wilson G. *Your Brain on Porn: Internet Pornography and the Emerging Science of Addiction.* Commonwealth Publishing, 2015.

INTERNET

Kuss DJ, Griffiths MD. *Internet Addiction in Psychotherapy.* Palgrave Pivot, 2014.
Young KS. *Caught in the Net: How to Recognize the Signs of Internet Addiction.* Wiley, 1998.

FOOD

Kessler D. *The End of Overeating.* Rodale Books, 2012.
Riley G. *Eating Less: Say Goodbye to Overeating.* Vermilion, 2005.

SHOPPING AND BUYING

Benson AL. *To Buy or Not to Buy: Why We Overshop and How to Stop.* Trumpeter Books, 2009.
Muller A, Mitchell JE. *Compulsive Buying: Clinical Foundations and Treatment.* Routledge, 2011.

HAIR PULLING AND SKIN PICKING

Grant JE, Stein DJ, Woods DW, Keuthen NJ. *Trichotillomania, Skin Picking, and Other Body Focused Repetitive Behaviors.* APPI, 2011.
Keuthen NJ, Stein DJ, Christenson GA. *Help for Hair Pullers: Understanding and Coping with Trichotillomania.* New Harbinger, 2001.
Penzel F. *The Hair-Pulling Problem: A Complete Guide to Trichotillomania.* Oxford University Press, 2003.

NEUROBIOLOGY AND CAUSES OF BEHAVIORAL ADDICTIONS

Fineberg NA, Chamberlain SR, Goudriaan AE, Stein DJ, et al. New developments in human neurocognition: clinical, genetic, and brain imaging correlates of impulsivity and compulsivity. *CNS Spectrums* 2014 Feb;19(1):69–89.
Grant JE, Potenza MN, Weinstein A, Gorelick DA. Introduction to behavioral addictions. *American Journal of Drug and Alcohol Abuse* 2010 Sep;36(5):233–41.
Potenza MN. The neural bases of cognitive processes in gambling disorder. *Trends in Cognitive Sciences* 2014 Aug;18(8):429–38.

INDEX

adolescents (and children): age at onset in, 16, 61, 90, 153; brain development in, 176; comorbidity in, 108; diagnosis of, 61; presentation in, 173–74; prevalence in, 38–39, 61, 103, 105; social factors in, 18, 44, 61, 68–69, 92, 124, 134, 169–70, 194, 201; treatment of, 112, 115, 128, 160, 162, 190

age at onset: in compulsive buying, 139–40; in compulsive sexual behavior, 90, 92; in food addiction, 122; in gambling, 39, 44; in kleptomania, 60–61; in skin-picking, 153; in trichotillomania, 153

alcohol misuse: co-occurrence with behavioral addictions, 16, 24, 64, 154; family history of, 18, 29, 41–42, 72, 140, 156

antidepressants, 23, 50–51, 75, 98, 112, 145, 163

antipsychotics, 42, 51, 162–63

anxiety: co-occurrence with behavioral addictions, 35–37, 62–63, 82, 84, 110, 123, 138, 154, 163, 171–72; distinguishing behavioral addictions from, 21–24; effects of behaviors on, 15, 68, 83, 141, 173

behavioral addictions: clinical similarities of, 14–16; definition of, 8; general prevalence of, 13; general problems with control in, 1–2, 8, 14–15; grouping of, 11–12; history of, 4; labeling of, 8; misdiagnosis of, 23, 66, 159

biological understanding: brain imaging, of, 9, 19, 30, 70, 107, 141–42, 175–83; dopamine, of, 18–19, 42, 70; genetics, of, 10, 18, 29, 41–42, 91–92, 106–7, 126, 140, 156–57, 169–71; glutamate, of, 19, 21, 42, 51, 162; serotonin, of, 19, 43, 70, 127, 141; ventral striatum, of the, 14, 69, 108, 142, 157, 176–83

bipolar disorder: co-occurrence of behavioral addictions with, 23, 37, 63, 88; distinguishing behavioral addictions from, 23–24, 40–41, 66, 88, 136–37

body image: food addiction and, 124–25; sex addiction and, 96–97; skin picking and trichotillomania and, 155

brain imaging studies. *See* biological understanding

compulsive shopping and buying: alternative explanations for, 136–37; alternatives to treatment for, 146–47; antidepressants for, 145; case example of, 131–32, 147–48; clinical aspects of, 135–37; consequences of, 132–33, 138–39;

compulsive shopping and buying (*cont.*)
Debtors Anonymous for, 144; development of, 140; diagnosis of, 133–35;
financial counseling treatment for, 145;
gender and, 139; goals of treatment for,
146; medications for, 144–45; memantine for, 145; naltrexone for, 145;
neurobiology of, 140–42; onset of,
139–40; prevalence of, 132, 139;
psychotherapy for, 143–44; recognition
of, 134–35; support groups for, 144;
transference of addiction in, 145–46
cognitive behavioral therapy, 20, 47–49,
73–74, 94–95, 111–12, 127–28, 143–44
compulsive exercise, 5, 13
co-occurrence (comorbidity): anxiety
disorders, with, 23, 35, 37, 62–63, 68, 82,
84, 110, 123, 159, 171; mood disorders,
with, 21–23, 35–36, 62, 66, 82, 84, 110,
123, 154, 172; obsessive compulsive
disorder, with, 21–23, 67, 141, 155;
substance addiction, with, 16–17, 24, 29,
35, 62–63, 67, 82, 84–85, 110, 172–73
craving, 14–15, 121, 127, 175

depression: gender differences in, 171–72;
misdiagnosis of behavioral addictions
as, 22–24, 82, 110, 136; relationship to
behavioral addictions, 36, 68, 71, 83, 123
diagnosis of behavioral addictions:
misdiagnosis, 23–24, 66–68, 136–37;
screening questions, 31–32, 58–59,
82–83, 105, 122, 135, 152
*Diagnostic and Statistical Manual of Mental
Disorders*, fifth edition (*DSM-5*), 5, 10,
20, 58, 81, 104, 121, 134, 150
diet and nutrition, 126–27, 169, 175, 183
dopamine. *See* biological understanding
drug abuse: co-occurrence with behavioral
addictions and, 35–36, 84–85, 138; family
history of, 18, 23–24, 41–42, 67–68,
91–92, 106–7, 126, 140–42, 156–57

eating disorders, 63–64, 97, 119–21, 174
elderly, 39, 45, 154, 205

family history, 18, 50, 106–7, 113, 140,
156–57, 163, 180
family relationships and behavioral
addictions: empathy in, 187–88; enabling
behavior in, 188; parent and child
dynamics in, 188–89; perspective of,
186–87; problems with, 191–98;
reluctance to get treatment on, effects of,
195–96; suicidal thinking on, effects of,
197–98; treatment by, support of,
189–91
fire setting, 5, 13
food addiction: case example of, 118–19,
128–29; clinical concerns in, 119–20;
co-occurring health and mental health
problems in, 122–24; development of,
125–26; diagnosis of, 121–22; genetics
of, 126; health consequences in, 122–23;
history of, 120–21; medications for, 128;
neurobiology of, 126–27; outcomes in,
122; prevalence of, 120; psychological
consequences in, 122–24; psychotherapy
for, 127–28; underdiagnosis of, 124–25

gambling disorder: age at onset of, 39;
antidepressants for, 50–51; binges in,
33; case example of, 26, 28, 54; clinical
concerns in, 29; cognitive behavior
therapy for, 47; consequences of, 33–34;
co-occurring health and mental health
issues in, 35–37; cue exposure for, 49;
culture and, 39; diagnosis of, 30, 40–41;
DSM-5 and, 29; family involvement in,
30; financial consequences in, 34;
Gamblers Anonymous for, 50; gambling
patterns in, 32; gender and, 38; genetics
and, 29, 41–42; group therapy for, 49;
imaginal desensitization for, 49; lithium
for, 51; medications for, 50–51; mental
health consequences in, 35–37;
N-acetylcysteine for, 43, 51; naltrexone
for, 50–51; natural recovery in, 45;
neurobiology of, 42–43; physical health
consequences in, 35; positive affirma-
tions and, 47–48; prevalence of, 37;

privacy issues in, 30; problem gambling and, 33; psychological factors in, 43–44; psychotherapy for, 46–48; residential treatment for, 49–50; severity levels in, 32; social and environmental factors in, 44; special issues in treatment for, 52–53; substance addiction and, 35–36; suicidality in, 36; symptoms of, 30–32; treatment for, 44–51; treatment goals in, 45–46; triggers in, 49

gambling industry, 29

gender differences, 16, 38–39, 57, 60, 64, 89, 90–91, 106, 120, 139, 171–73

glutamate. *See* biological understanding

grooming disorders. *See* skin picking; trichotillomania

group therapy, 49, 95, 112

hair-pulling. *See* trichotillomania

Internet addiction: alternative explanations for, 108–9; alternatives to treatment for, 114–15; case example of, 102–3, 116–17; clinical aspects of, 106; clinical importance of, 103; consequences of, 109–11; development of, 106–7; diagnosis of, 104–5; differentiation of, 104; goals of treatment for, 114; Internet and Tech Addiction Anonymous (ITAA) for, 113; medications for, 112; neurobiology of, 107–8; On-Line Gamers Anonymous (OLGA) for, 113; prevalence of, 105; prevention of, 115–16; psychotherapy for, 111–12; residential treatment for, 112–13; support groups for, 113–14

isolation, feelings of, 110, 196–97, 203

major depression. *See* depression

manic-depressive illness. *See* bipolar disorder

medications. *See specific behaviors*

memantine, 21, 75, 145

morals, 11–12, 25–26, 189

motivational enhancement (interviewing), 20, 48, 52, 74, 143

N-acetylcysteine (NAC), 21, 43, 51, 128, 162, 164

nail-biting, 5, 13, 150, 156, 206

naltrexone, 21, 50–51, 70, 75, 98, 113, 128, 145, 163

noradrenaline. *See* biological understanding

nymphomania. *See* sex addiction

Obsessive Compulsive and Related Disorders, 10, 151

obsessive compulsive disorder (OCD): co-occurrence of, 17, 155–56; misdiagnosis of behavioral addictions as, 67, 155, 159, 163; similarities to behavioral addictions, 21–23, 67, 141, 151, 155–56

olanzapine, 42, 51, 162, 164

oniomania, 4

opioid system. *See* biological understanding

Parkinson's disease, 20, 41, 70, 88, 92, 182

personality, in behavioral addictions, 16, 22, 24–25

relapse prevention, 21, 97

relationships, effects of behavioral addictions on, 2, 34, 62, 82, 87, 124, 186, 194, 199, 202

ritualistic behaviors, 22, 159, 191

satyrism, 4

secrecy, underdiagnosis of behavioral addictions, 65, 125

selective serotonin reuptake inhibitors. *See specific behaviors*

self-esteem, 44, 89, 91, 124, 153, 202

self-help groups, 20, 48, 50, 127, 144, 161

self-medication, 23, 72

serotonin. *See* biological understanding

sex addiction: age at onset of, 90; alternative explanations for, 87–88; antiandrogens for, 98; antidepressants for, 98; case example of, 79, 100; clinical aspects of,